FIFTY MORE PLACES TO FLY FISH

BEFORE YOU DIE

FIFTY MORE PLACES TO

FLY FISH

BEFORE YOU DIE

Fly-fishing Experts Share More of the World's Greatest Destinations

Chris Santella

FOREWORD BY KEN MORRISH

STEWART, TABORI & CHANG

NEW YORK

This book is for my girls, Cassidy, Annabel, and Deidre,
and the waters that I hope we'll one day fish together . . . or at least read a book by!

Fifty Places to Fly Fish Before You Die:
Fly-Fishing Experts Share the World's Greatest Destinations

Fifty Places to Play Golf Before You Die:
Golf Experts Share the World's Greatest Destinations

Fifty Favorite Fly-Fishing Tales:
Expert Fly Anglers Share Stories from the Sea and Stream

Fifty Places to Sail Before You Die:
Sailing Experts Share the World's Greatest Destinations

Fifty Places to Go Birding Before You Die:
Birding Experts Share the World's Greatest Destinations

Fifty Places to Dive Before You Die:
Diving Experts Share the World's Greatest Destinations

Fifty Places to Hike Before You Die:
Outdoor Experts Share the World's Greatest Destinations

Once in a Lifetime Trips:
The World's 50 Most Extraordinary and Memorable Travel Experiences

Fifty More Places to Play Golf Before You Die:
Golf Experts Share the World's Greatest Destinations

Contents

Acknowledgments 9 / Foreword 10 / Introduction 11

THE DESTINATIONS

(1) **Alaska–Kodiak Island:** Karluk River 17
RECOMMENDED BY KIRK DEETER

(2) **Alaska–Quinhagak:** Kanektok River 21
RECOMMENDED BY ANDREW BENNETT

(3) **Alberta:** Bow River 25
RECOMMENDED BY MIKE GIFFORD

(4) **Argentina:** Jurassic Lake 29
RECOMMENDED BY CHRISTER SJÖBERG

(5) **Australia–Cape York:** Gulf of Carpentaria 33
RECOMMENDED BY GREG BETHUNE

(6) **Australia–Tasmania:** Central Highlands 37
RECOMMENDED BY KEN ORR

(7) **Belize–Mainland:** Punta Gorda 43
RECOMMENDED BY JIM KLUG

(8) **Belize–Offshore:** Turneffe Atoll 47
RECOMMENDED BY STEVE ABEL

(9) **Bolivia:** Asunta and Pluma Rivers 51
RECOMMENDED BY BRIAN GIES

(10) **British Columbia–Omineca Mountains:** Sustut River 55
RECOMMENDED BY KEN MORRISH

(11) **British Columbia–West Kootenay:** Columbia River 58
RECOMMENDED BY GEOFF MUELLER

(12) **California:** San Diego 61
RECOMMENDED BY CONWAY BOWMAN

(13) **Chile:** Rio Cisnes 65
RECOMMENDED BY TIM PURVIS

(14) **Colorado–Denver:** South Platte River 69
RECOMMENDED BY WILL RICE

15   **Colorado–Pagosa Springs:** Rio Blanco 73
      RECOMMENDED BY JIM HILL

16   **England:** Derbyshire Wye 76
      RECOMMENDED BY DR. JOHN SMITH

17   **Florida:** Homosassa Springs 79
      RECOMMENDED BY MAC MCKEEVER

18   **Guatemala:** Puerto San José 83
      RECOMMENDED BY CHUCK FURIMSKY

19   **Hawaii:** Oahu 88
      RECOMMENDED BY MIKE HENNESSY

20   **Iceland–Akureyri:** Upper Laxá I Adaldal 93
      RECOMMENDED BY PETER MCLEOD

21   **Iceland–Hvammstang:** Miðfjarðará River 97
      RECOMMENDED BY APRIL VOKEY

22   **Idaho–Driggs:** South Fork of the Snake 101
      RECOMMENDED BY RANDY BERRY

23   **Idaho–Ketchum/Sun Valley:** Silver Creek 105
      RECOMMENDED BY BOB UNNASCH

24   **India:** Western Ramganga River 109
      RECOMMENDED BY JEFF CURRIER

25   **Ireland:** River Moy 115
      RECOMMENDED BY JOE HEALY

26   **Maine:** Casco Bay 119
      RECOMMENDED BY ERIC WALLACE

27   **Mexico–Baja California Sur:** East Cape 123
      RECOMMENDED BY JAD DONALDSON

28   **Mexico–Yucatán:** Costa Maya 128
      RECOMMENDED BY BILL MARTS

29   **Montana:** Big Hole River 133
      RECOMMENDED BY DENISE SCHREIBER

30   **New Brunswick:** Miramichi River 137
      RECOMMENDED BY BILL TAYLOR

31   **Newfoundland and Labrador:** Hawke River 141
      RECOMMENDED BY MIKE CROSBY

32   **North Carolina:** Cape Lookout 145
      RECOMMENDED BY JAKE JORDAN

33 **North Carolina/Tennessee:** Great Smoky Mountains National Park 149
RECOMMENDED BY IAN RUTTER

34 **Norway:** Målselv River 153
RECOMMENDED BY MARK HEWETSON-BROWN

35 **Oregon–Camp Sherman:** Metolius River 157
RECOMMENDED BY JOHN JUDY

36 **Oregon–Condon:** John Day River 163
RECOMMENDED BY MARTY SHEPPARD

37 **Seychelles:** Outer Atolls 167
RECOMMENDED BY HENRY GILBEY

38 **Slovenia:** Soča River 171
RECOMMENDED BY ROK LUSTRIK

39 **South Africa:** Vaal River 175
RECOMMENDED BY GERHARD LAUBSCHER

40 **Texas–Gulf Coast:** Port O'Connor 179
RECOMMENDED BY KEVIN TOWNSHEND

41 **Texas–Hill Country:** Llano River 183
RECOMMENDED BY TIM ROMANO

42 **Texas–South Padre Island:** Laguna Madre 187
RECOMMENDED BY ERIC GLASS

43 **Venezuela:** Los Roques 191
RECOMMENDED BY JOEL LA FOLLETTE

44 **Wales:** Rivers Teifi and Towy 195
RECOMMENDED BY STEFFAN JONES

45 **Washington, DC:** Middle Potomac River 199
RECOMMENDED BY MIKE BAILEY

46 **Washington–Kalaloch:** Queets River 203
RECOMMENDED BY MIKE DICKSON

47 **Washington–Seattle:** Puget Sound 209
RECOMMENDED BY DAVE MCCOY

48 **Wisconsin–Fennimore to Hudson:** The Driftless Region 212
RECOMMENDED BY DR. GARY BORGER

49 **Wisconsin–Northwoods:** Greater Hayward 215
RECOMMENDED BY ROBERT TOMES

50 **Wyoming/Colorado:** Upper North Platte River 221
RECOMMENDED BY JOHN LAND LE COQ

ACKNOWLEDGMENTS

This book would not have been possible without the generous assistance of the expert anglers who shared their time and experience to help bring these fifty great fishing locales to life. To these men and women, I offer the most heartfelt thanks. I would especially like to thank Mac McKeever and Ken Morrish, who both offered encouragement and made many introductions on my behalf. I also wish to acknowledge the fine efforts of my agent, Stephanie Kip Rostan, my editors Wesley Royce and Jennifer Levesque, designer Anna Christian, and copyeditor Ashley Benning who helped bring the book into being. I've had the good fortune over the last thirty years to make many fine fishing friends who have furthered my horizons, both in terms of angling experiences and a greater appreciation of life. This list includes Howard Kyser, Peter Marra, Ken Matsumoto, Jeff Sang, Joe Runyon, Mark Harrison, Peter Gyerko, Tim Purvis, Geoff Roach, Kenton Quist, Mike Marcus, John Smith, David Moscowitz, Ken Helm, Bryce Tedford, Darrell Hanks, and Hamp Byerly. I look forward to many more days on the river with these friends and friends to come. A special thanks goes to Paul Franklin and WaterWatch, on behalf of the group's fine efforts to keep rivers flowing in my native Oregon. I also extend kudos to Sloan Morris, Keith Carlson, and Doug Mateer, who've helped put fly fishing to music in our band, Catch & Release.

Finally, I want to extend a special thanks to my wife, Deidre, and my daughters, Cassidy and Annabel, who've humored my absence on far too many occasions so I could pursue my favorite pastime . . . and to my parents, who are not anglers, but always encouraged me to pursue my passions.

FOREWORD

Having spent my entire working life in the fly-fishing industry and the past twelve years happily immersed in international fly-fishing travel, I am one of the first to applaud works that highlight the pleasures of fishing new and sometimes distant waters. It is a broad field with an unfathomable number of venues and outfitters, not all of which are created equal. Sorting through these many options in search of the true gems is an ongoing process and a challenge I enjoy. In the same breath, I know that to do it well takes a lot of work and energy, making me all the more impressed when an author can take a topic of diversity and distil it into something as balanced, informative, and inspiring as Chris Santella's *Fifty More Places to Fly Fish Before You Die*. This man clearly did his homework.

Both fly fishing and travel demand a need for adventure, interest in the natural sciences, athleticism, and, above all else, an innate and irrepressible obsession for which there is no cure. When it comes to fly fishing in its purest form, and a discussion of the "World's Greatest" fishing destinations, there will never be consensus. There are no formulas, nor absolute truths. Instead, we face a myriad of subtle choices that, on rare occasions, combine with good fortune to create fishing scenarios so special we cannot help but consider them among the most exciting and pleasurable of our earthly experiences. Though anglers may not reach consensus on the perfect "bucket list," this volume certainly offers something for everyone—from the choosy trout of Idaho's Silver Creek to Tasmania's fabled tarns, the less than particular giant trevally of the Seychelles' Outer Atolls, and the giant rainbows of Argentina's Jurassic Lake.

For fly anglers, it is this hope of being in the right place at the right time that helps us through the motions of our daily grind, wakes us happily before dawn, and compels us to travel to the far corners of the globe. It is also the inspiration for this book, an impressive collection of dream trips, carefully selected to help all those with the burning drive to travel and fish make the most of their cherished time on the water.

—Ken Morrish, Fly Water Travel

INTRODUCTION

In 2003, I was fortunate enough to realize a lifelong dream—to have a chance to write a book. Better yet, it was to be a fly-fishing book, a topic dear to my heart, and it would be titled *Fifty Places to Fly Fish Before You Die*. My thinking at the time was that this would be my one book—something every writer I know hopes to achieve—and that I'd return to my marketing-consulting practice once it was done and have something neat to show my grandchildren (the book, that is).

Thanks largely to the book's beautiful design and to the wonderful angling insights the fifty individuals I interviewed provided, *Fifty Places to Fly Fish Before You Die* was far more successful than anyone could have imagined. Not quit-my-day-job-and-buy-a-fishing-lodge successful, but successful enough that I was offered the opportunity to write another book . . . and another book . . . and another . . . and now this, my tenth title—*Fifty More Places to Fly Fish Before You Die*—truly a labor of love!

At bookstore readings and fly-fishing club meetings, audience members often ask, "Did you go to all of these fifty places, and if you did, how can I get that job?" I must sadly answer no. While I have been fortunate enough to do a bit of angling travel (mostly around North America), the fifty places in this new book have been compiled by interviewing people from around the angling world and asking them to chat about an angling venue that's unique, a place that's dear to their heart, a place that . . . well, that you need to fly fish before you go off to the great streams and flats of the hereafter. As a writer who often covers travel-oriented topics, I have the opportunity to visit frequently with many very well-traveled anglers, folks who have had a chance to experience "the next big thing." A few such places certainly appear in this book (like the clear-flowing golden dorado rivers of Bolivia and the roosterfish beaches of Baja California), but there are also some old favorites that anglers have been returning to again and again for generations (Idaho's Silver Creek and New Brunswick's Miramichi, to name a few). Some venues are smack-dab in the middle of sprawling urban areas (like the South Platte in Denver or the Bow in Calgary); others (like the Outer Atolls of the Seychelles or Cape York, Australia) are so remote that you're not likely to encounter anyone there beyond your party. All, I believe, provide a window into what makes fly anglers tick, what excites us, and how place informs our experience of this pastime.

While this book collects fifty great fly-fishing experiences, it by no means attempts to rank the waters discussed or the quality of the experiences these fisheries afford. Such ranking is entirely subjective—one angler's passion might be another's bane. To dispel any notions of preference, the fifty venues are listed alphabetically. In the hope that a few readers might decide to embark on adventures of their own, I have provided some "If You Go" information at the end of each section. It is by no means exhaustive but will give would-be travelers a starting point for planning their trip. I've also included some tackle tips, to give you a sense of what you'll need to bring along . . . and what new fly rods you'll just have to buy!

While I write for a living and so certainly hope to sell books, I must say that the greatest satisfaction I've received from my writing has not been from a royalty check, but from the kind words of a stranger I might run into on a river or in a bookstore or via e-mail who has picked up the book (or received it as a gift) and found it enjoyable—and even in a few cases, inspirational. (I've had more than one person tell me that he plans to visit all fifty and is keeping a checklist!) I hope this little book provides you with a mini fly-fishing adventure for each chapter you read and with a few ideas for future, full-blown angling expeditions that you can share with your best fishing buddies.

OPPOSITE:
A fall angler on British Columbia's Sustut, where any cast could connect you with a "super-tanker" steelhead.

NEXT PAGE:
Searching for bonefish along the shoreline of a cay at Los Roques, Venezuela.

The Destinations

KARLUK RIVER

RECOMMENDED BY **Kirk Deeter**

"I've made many trips to Alaska in my time as a fishing writer," Kirk Deeter began. "It's a sprawling and multifaceted place, the size of the United States east of the Mississippi. In recent years, I've become enamored with Kodiak Island. Though Kodiak is just the size of Connecticut, many of my favorite attributes of Alaska are there—rugged mountains, fjords, glaciers, tundra, and, of course, pristine rivers. It's the home of the Kodiak brown bear, an iconic, majestic apex predator, the great white shark of the land. The weather changes frequently and dramatically, and this creates an ever-evolving landscape. You never know what you'll find when you fly over a mountain to a river or estuary. Because of this, everyone—from pilots to sea captains to guides—has to really stay on top of things. I've gotten to know a lot of Alaskan guides over the years, and many of them come over to Kodiak to fish when their work season is done. That says a lot."

Kodiak Island rests 17 miles across the Shelikof Strait from the Alaska Peninsula, and 265 air miles from Anchorage. It's a wild, remote place, even by Alaska standards. The topography is defined by rugged mountains, cut through by hundreds of fjord-like sounds. The island has only 100 miles of road to accommodate its fourteen thousand citizens. For many here, a fly-fishing excursion—or an errand to pick up a half gallon of milk—necessitates a jaunt in a floatplane—and the de Havilland DHC-2 Beaver is the craft of choice. "The Beaver has the capacity to haul large loads, and it has excellent STOL [short take off and landing] characteristics," said Jay Wattum, a bush pilot at Kodiak Legends Lodge. "That's essential when you're going into hazardous places like mountain lakes where you need to get up and down fast." Only 1,657 Beavers were manufactured by de Havilland Canada, the last in 1967. Prized for their dependability, a forty- or fifty-year-old aircraft still goes for half a million dollars.

OPPOSITE:
Most anglers
reach the Karluk
via floatplane,
and more often
than not, the
craft of choice is
the de Havilland
DHC-2 Beaver.

The fishing possibilities the Beaver opens up on Kodiak Island are impressive. There are rainbows eager to take mouse patterns on the Upper Dog Salmon River, fresh from the sea silver salmon in Brown's Lagoon and Zachar Bay, and Dolly Varden in nearly every creek that feeds the region's many lakes. "I've been up in the Beaver for five hours at a time, exploring different streams out of Larsen Bay," said Trent Deeter, head guide at Kodiak Legends Lodge. "We landed on ten different drainages, and every one had salmon and Dollies in them. From a fishing perspective, the waters of Kodiak are still largely unexplored. Many of the streams and creeks don't even have a name."

Kodiak's most celebrated fishery is the Karluk, which flows 25 miles from Karluk Lake to the Pacific. The river hosts all five species of Pacific salmon, as well as resident Dollies and a smattering of rainbows. Many come to fish for silvers, which arrive in mid-August and can run to 20 pounds. In October, the Karluk sees a rarity for these parts—a healthy run of wild steelhead, and this may be the river's greatest attraction for fly anglers. "The Karluk is relatively short by Alaska standards, crystal clear by Alaska standards, and shallow by almost anyone's standards," Kirk continued. "You can wade across just about anywhere. It has few of the qualities one associates with most Pacific Northwest steelhead waters—big, fast water, treacherous wading, etc. There's an abundance of fish [returns average around 8,000], which translates into an abundance of opportunity. But despite the shallow conditions, it's challenging fishing. The holding areas are not obvious; you have to find subtle distinctions in what seems like an endless riffle. I think it ups your game. Being able to read the nuances distinguishes good anglers from great anglers."

Fishing days on the Karluk (weather permitting) begin with a short floatplane ride over Larsen Bay and a ridge that separates the bay from the river. "One of the fundamental rules of fishing is 'the further afield, the better,'" Kirk offered. "If you're coming to Larsen Bay from the Lower 48, you're looking at least four flights—plus the floatplane into the river. You're about as far afield in a salmon/steelhead environment as you can be in North America, yet there's a safe plane and a warm bed to return to each night. And every steelhead you catch on the Karluk has an adipose fin, which is pretty cool." There are some pools on the Karluk where anglers can swing a fly in a traditional down-and-across presentation, but the most effective method of fishing is with an egg pattern or TroutBead below an indicator. "I do a lot of nymph fishing for trout in Colorado," Kirk added, "and this prepared me well for the steelheading on the Karluk." That may be a bit of an understatement, given a special October day that Kirk enjoyed.

"My last trip to Kodiak was over the first week in October. Our last day of fishing happened to be on October 10, 2010—that is, 10-10-10. I'd had pretty amazing fishing the day before, eight or nine fish to hand. When the Beaver landed on the Karluk that morning, it occurred to me that I'd only be on the planet on 10-10-10 once, and wouldn't it be quite a life experience to catch ten steelhead on this day. It certainly was in my mind that I was about to fish on perhaps the one river in the world where it wouldn't be too much of a stretch to catch ten steelhead—ten wild steelhead—in one day. The fish gods were with me, and without even fishing very hard, I had my tenth steelhead by lunchtime. Toasting the experience with the other guys I was fishing with, it sank in that I'd just had an experience that would be pretty tough to top: the perfect 10!"

KIRK DEETER is an editor at large for *Field & Stream* magazine and coeditor of its *Fly Talk* weblog. He is also the editor in chief of *Angling Trade* and senior editor of the *Flyfish Journal*. His stories have appeared in *Garden & Gun, The Drake, 5280, Fly Rod & Reel, Fly Fisherman, Big Sky Journal, SaltWater Sportsman*, and *Trout*, among other places. Kirk is also the coauthor of three books: *The Little Red Book of Fly Fishing* with Charlie Meyers; *Castworks: Reflections of Fly Fishing Guides and the American West* (Game & Fish Mastery Library) with Andrew W. Steketee and Liz Steketee; and *Tideline: Captains, Fly-Fishing and the American Coast* with Andrew W. Steketee and Marco Lorenzetti.

If You Go

▶ **Prime Time:** The steelhead season on the Karluk hits high gear in October. The annual silver run hits its peak in early September.

▶ **Getting There:** Karluk trips stage in the town of Kodiak, which is served (via Anchorage) by Alaska Airlines (800-252-7522; www.alaskaair.com). A charter flight takes you across the island to Larsen Bay, the village that's closest to the Karluk's best water.

▶ **Accommodations/Outfitters:** There are several lodges in the village of Larsen Bay. Kodiak Legends Lodge (877-563-4111; www.kodiaklegendslodge.com) is available for private rental.

▶ **Equipment:** A 7- or 8-weight single-handed rod outfitted with floating line will work well for silvers or steelhead on the Karluk.

KANEKTOK RIVER

RECOMMENDED BY **Andrew Bennett**

Among Alaska's angling cognoscenti, the Kanektok has long enjoyed a stellar reputation for its seclusion, scenery, and angling. For years, insiders simply referred to the Kanektok as "The Chosen." The river flows roughly 100 miles from its source at Pegati Lake, coursing westward between the Kilbuck and Ahklun Mountains and the tundra of the Togiak National Wildlife Refuge before meeting the Bering Sea. Fish encountered here include Dolly Varden, arctic char, all five species of Pacific salmon, and perhaps most famously, "leopard" rainbow trout, so nicknamed for their fine round spots.

Andrew Bennett had heard stories about the Kanektok, but he'd never fished it . . . until he purchased a sportfishing operation there. "An opportunity to get involved with Alaska West [which operates a fixed-base tent lodge in the lower river] came up," Andrew began. "Unfortunately, it was in November. I had to either buy the operation sight unseen, or wait until the spring . . . and I didn't think it would still be available come spring. I talked to a number of people who I trusted who had spent time at Alaska West and the Kanektok. They all said the fishery was exceptional, a unique place. I ended up buying the operation, and I wasn't disappointed. The Kanektok has tremendous species diversity, like some of the other Bristol Bay rivers. But it's too far from the fleet of Beavers (bush planes) that fly out for day trips from the lodges over there. When you're on the Kanektok, you don't have it to yourself. But it's *mostly* to yourself."

There are several ways to experience the bounties of the Kanektok. There are three base camps in the lower 50 miles of the river. Guests here motor up- or downriver (depending on what species they're seeking) and return to the relative comforts of a fixed-base tent lodge, with heated tents, hot running water for showers, and hearty cuisine. Though you won't find white linen tablecloths at the tent camps, accommodations exceed

OPPOSITE:
You can either
float down the
Kanektok from
its headwaters
or motor up from
one of the few
tent camps in
the lower half
of the river.
You won't be
hiking in!

most expectations for a venue in the middle of the Alaska bush. For those seeking more of an adventure, it's possible to float the length of the Kanektok over the course of a week. Guides will set up your camp each evening on a gravel bar (so the grizzlies can see you from afar), and your only worry is not exhausting yourself pulling in fish after fish. While not quite as coddled an experience as the base camps afford, a float allows you to watch a rich wilderness river system unfold as it moves from its headwaters through low mountains, braids into many smaller flows, and converges into a significant river as it moves to the salt. The biomass of the river is jaw-dropping, especially in even numbered years when pink salmon are returning; in its upper reaches, the Kanektok can be bank to bank with fish. As alluded to above, you're almost certain to see grizzly bears patrolling the shore for fish or roaming the hillsides for blueberries if you float the river. It's both awe-inspiring and mildly terrifying to see such animals, knowing there's no floatplane or jetboat nearby to spirit you away. Yet, their presence—along with caribou and the possibility of spying on (or at least hearing) gray wolves—adds a special dimension to the trip.

If you're feeling particularly adventurous (and are modestly confident in your outdoor skills), you can float the Kanektok yourself; an outfitter will rent you a raft, fly all your equipment in, and pick you up at the bottom, at the Yup'ik Eskimo village of Quinhagak. When the Beaver flies off from Pegati Lake and your group is left with your raft, you feel *very* alone.

Untrammeled wilderness and large bears aside, it is the fishing that brings most visitors to the Kanektok, and there is truly something for everyone. Wherever there are salmon spawning, or just about anywhere else, you can tie on a TroutBead above a Gamakatsu Octopus hook and catch Dollies and arctic char in the 18- to 22-inch range as long as you wish—the kind of angling fun you'd drive across your home state to enjoy in the Lower 48. A TroutBead—or, as you move into the later summer and farther downriver, a flesh fly—will also attract the K's rainbows—hands down, one of the most beautiful salmonids in the world, with rich reds and oranges, a hint of vermillion, and thousands of fine spots. "The thing I love about the Kanektok as a rainbow fishery is the great variety in terms of where we fish, how we fish, and even the fish we catch," Andrew continued. "It's not the type of program where if you get the nail polish wrong on your bead, you're not getting fish. You can fish sculpins, flesh, or mice, work big snags for bigger fish, sight-fish along the side channels and fish below salmon spawning beds for numbers. The fish have many unique looks; I'm always eager to get them to the boat to see what kind of makeup they've put on. I tell people that if they want to catch a 30-inch rainbow, there are better places to go—but we have them. Mousing can be a great way to bring up the bigger fish. They'll move a long distance to get such a big piece of protein. When you see a torpedo coming at your mouse from 20 feet away, it's hard not to yank the fly away before it gets its mouth around it. The first time it happens, most anglers do."

The salmon species that return to the Kanektok all have their appeals. For Andrew, the kings (or chinook) have the greatest, especially when they're fresh from the salt. "In most Alaskan rivers, you're dealing with a volume of water and a river structure that doesn't lend itself well to swinging flies—or, by the time you get to water where you can effectively swing a fly, you're so far upriver that the fish aren't fresh and are lock-jawed. Try swinging a fly in the lower Kenai—it's like fishing the Mississippi with a 3-weight!

"The bottom 9 miles of the Kanektok have perfect structure for swinging flies. Any of the gravel bars work. The closer to the salt, the greater the propensity for the kings to eat a swung fly. It's like winter steelhead fishing—yank, yank, *yank*—except the fish are more plentiful, and they're bigger. We have lots of fish in the teens, a fair number in the 20s; in a week of fishing, you'll probably get a 30-pounder, and there will generally be one 50-pounder at the camp each season. It's not a numbers fishery—a few fish to hand is a good day. A majority of our anglers are using spey rods for kings. During the king season, we run a spey-casting instruction program for anyone interested in learning this effective technique for covering big water with big flies."

ANDREW BENNETT grew up in Fairbanks, Alaska, with a strong love for the outdoors. After spending some time in the software industry, he founded Deneki Outdoors to build a business that combined his passion for fly fishing with beautiful places and great people. Deneki Outdoors owns and operates four fly-fishing lodges: Alaska West on the Kanektok River in Alaska, BC West on the Dean River in British Columbia, Andros South on South Andros Island in the Bahamas, and Chile West in Chilean Patagonia. Andrew lives in Seattle but spends several months on-site at his lodges throughout the year.

If You Go

▶ **Prime Time:** The Kanektok fishes from mid-June through mid-September. The chinook fishery is at its height the first month of the season; silvers fish best the last month. Rainbows fish well throughout.

▶ **Getting There:** Kanektok trips stage in Bethel, which is served (via Anchorage) by Alaska Airlines (800-252-7522; www.alaskaair.com). A charter flight takes you in to either the mouth or the headwaters.

▶ **Guides/Outfitters:** For guided trips, there are two options: Alaska West (800-344-3628; www.deneki.com) and Dave Duncan & Sons (509-962-1060; www.alaskafly fishingcamps.com), both operate tent camps on the lower half of the river. Duncan & Sons also leads guided floats. For intrepid outdoors people who want to go it alone, PaPa Bear Adventures (907-543-5275; www.pbadventures.com) will fly you in and out and rent you everything you need . . . including bear mace.

▶ **Equipment:** For rainbows: a 6-weight rod with floating line and a mini-sink tip will cover most situations. For kings: a 9- or 10-weight spey rod with Skagit-style lines *or* a 10- to 12-weight 9-foot single-hand rod with shooting heads and a range of sink tips; reels should have 200 yards of backing. For silvers: an 8-weight rod with floating and T-200 lines and a reel with 150 yards of backing will suffice. Your outfitter will provide you with a fly list.

BOW RIVER

RECOMMENDED BY **Mike Gifford**

"I was born in Calgary, Alberta, and when I started fly fishing at age ten or eleven, the Bow was my local river," Mike Gifford began. "For me, it was a bike ride away. As I began fishing other streams around Alberta on camping trips with my family, I began to realize how special the Bow was. Thirty years later, I'm still enthralled by this anomalous river."

The Bow River flows 387 miles in a southeasterly direction from its headwaters at Bow Glacier, north of Lake Louise in Banff National Park. In its upper reaches, the Bow has all the trappings of a classic alpine trout stream—conifer-lined banks, gravelly riffles, sweeping backdrops of vertiginous mountains, and a slightly off-color tint that suggests cover for lunkers lurking just below the surface. But appearances can be deceiving. While the upper Bow does hold trout, its icy, glacier-fed waters do not sustain fish in large numbers.

East from Banff, the Canadian Rockies give way to rolling hills and then prairie. Not long after the mountains are left behind, the western edges of Calgary begin to come into a view. Once a quiet city on the edge of the plains with once-a-year notoriety for the world's largest rodeo, Calgary has nearly tripled in size in the last forty years to over a million residents; this, thanks to an oil boom, a winter Olympics hosting coup (in 1988), and its outdoors-oriented lifestyle. The Bow River bifurcates Calgary as it rolls toward its junction with the South Saskatchewan River, ultimately reaching Hudson Bay. Generally speaking, the demands and detritus of a budding metropolis spell death (or at least considerable degradation) for a trout stream. But in the case of the Bow, Calgary's swelling population—and more specifically, its wastewater treatment needs—have helped create a world-class fishery in the 30-odd miles of river from the city east to the rural town of Carseland. Here, wild rainbow and brown trout *average* near 18 inches in length and browns stretching more than 25 inches are regularly encountered.

It is the infusion of nutrients into the Bow's clean, cold water from Calgary's two wastewater treatment plants that are most responsible for elevating the river to blue-ribbon status. The inflow—from car wash leftovers to bathroom water—goes through a four-stage treatment process. The effluent that's released back into the river is quite clean, though it has just enough phosphorus and nitrogen to foster an incredibly rich aquatic ecosystem. "The Bow River fishery has grown and improved as the city has grown," said Brian Meagher, a provincial biologist with Trout Unlimited Canada who works in Calgary. "Residents have come to recognize what we have here, and the fishery has evolved as people have become more conscious of the river.

"It's certainly unique to have a world-class trout fishery flowing through the middle of a metropolis," Mike continued. "I have caught trout over 2 feet in length in easy view of the skyscrapers of Calgary. Non-anglers are pretty accustomed to see fly fishers along the river corridor. We're part of the scenery, like people walking their dogs."

On the Bow, it's not inconceivable to hook the trout of a lifetime during your lunch break and be back at the office in time for the 2:00 P.M. Work-In-Progress update meeting!

The brown and rainbow trout that call the Bow home are not native to the river. Both were introduced in the 1920s; the browns reached the river when a truck carrying 45,000 fingerlings broke down near the river before reaching its intended destination, and the driver released them into the Bow, rather than see them perish. "In the city and the stretches immediately below, there are faster runs and riffles," Mike said. "This area is home to predominately browns, and generally the biggest browns the river yields come from within the city limits. There are times on city floats when you might think you're in the wild, the foliage along the banks is so thick. Then you'll come around a corner, and there are hillsides with one- and two-million-dollar houses. You might be casting a #16 Caddis as someone flips burgers on their deck. As you move downstream, the river loses some of its pitch. There are longer, slower runs as you head toward Carseland (the bottom end of the blue-ribbon section), and these lower sections mostly hold rainbows." The Bow at this point is a large river, from 100 yards across to nearly twice that size, moving past rolling prairie land dotted with copses of hardwoods and pines. (Many anglers will float the Bow, though numerous access points allow walk-and-wade fishers a chance to find good water.)

Beyond its consistently large trout, the Bow is renowned for its hatches (abetted by the aforementioned wastewater plants), which begin in earnest in early July. While the golden stonefly hatch may garner the most attention from casual anglers (who can resist big trout on big flies?), there are others that compete for Mike's fancy. "Early season caddis emergences provide a neat time to be on the river. At this time—and when the golden stones start coming off—there can also be prolific hatches of pale morning duns. The Trico hatch, which usually begins in late July or early August, is also special."

Like Mike, daughter Caity has grown up on the Bow, and he was privileged to be with her when she caught her first fish over 20 inches. "I was rowing the boat about 10 miles below town, and the golden stone hatch was on," Mike recalled. "Caity was casting a Chernobyl-style pattern. One cast brought up a big brown, and she did everything right—waited for the slow eat and stuck the fish once it had taken the bug. It was 24 inches, a heavy, perfectly colored brown. She was thirteen at the time.

"The following year, Caity returned the favor. She rowed me down the river while I fished hoppers. As special as it was to see my daughter get her first lunker, it was even more special to catch fish while Caity rowed."

MIKE GIFFORD has resided in southern Alberta for most of his life and has extensive experience fishing the Bow, the Crowsnest, and the waters of southeastern British Columbia. In the mid-1980s he began guiding anglers on the Bow River and now owns Country Pleasures Fly Shop. Mike has extensive experience in freshwater with trout, bass, and pike, and in salt water with such diverse species as tarpon, bonefish, and trevally.

If You Go

► **Prime Time:** The Bow from Calgary to Carseland is open to fishing year-round. The most famous hatches occur from late June through early August.
► **Getting There:** Calgary is served by many major carriers, including Air Canada (888-247-2262; www.aircanada.com) and Alaska Airlines (800-252-7522; www.alaskaair.com).
► **Accommodations:** Tourism Calgary (800-661-1678; www.tourismcalgary.com) lists the many lodging options available here.
► **Guides/Outfitters:** There are a number of guides and fly shops that service anglers on the Bow, including Country Pleasures (403-271-1016; www.countrypleasures.com).
► **Equipment:** A 5-weight rod equipped with a floating line will work for most situations. A local fly shop will help you identify the bugs that are working when you visit.

JURASSIC LAKE

RECOMMENDED BY **Christer Sjöberg**

On the barren Patagonian steppe, hundreds of miles southeast of the region's many renowned trout streams, rests an anomaly that's come to be known as Jurassic Lake. Those who've made the trek will likely tell you that it is, beyond a doubt, the most prolific rainbow trout fishery in the world.

"Back in 2004, I had some clients visiting the Loop lodge at Las Buitreras in southern Argentina, and they showed photos of these huge rainbows—10 pounds and more," Christer Sjöberg began. "I asked where they'd found these giants, and they said it was a lake to the north. I'd heard a bit about this lake, but had never thought much about it. Now I was curious. They said the only way to get there was by helicopter. I began to investigate this option, but there were too many complications—not to mention the challenge of taking off and landing in the Patagonian wind. Another year passed, and I decided that we should try to go and find it. I set up a little expedition, but at the last minute, I was unable to go. The others had the truck loaded, and I encouraged them to continue. It was not an easy journey. The roads were hardly roads, and the guys spent eight hours jumping over rocks and holes. They should've worn helmets, it was so bumpy. When they reached the estancia that contains the lake, the gaucho that made them dinner had the dirtiest fingers they'd ever seen. As they ate, wondering if they were going to be poisoned, they made up stories about different ways that they'd kill me when they got back.

"The next day, they drove through the estancia to the lake. They rigged up their rods, and in three hours caught seventy fish up to 20 pounds. Tim Pask was with the group, and he filmed some of their exploits. During the footage, you could hear him screaming, 'Swimming pigs! Swimming pigs!' By the time they left the lake, they wanted to kiss me. That might have been worse."

OPPOSITE:
The sun rises
on Jurassic Lake,
where the world-
record rainbow
trout may very
well wait.

Jurassic Lake (known to gazetteers as Lago Strobel) is a large desert sink lake approaching 300 square kilometers. The lake is rich in scuds and krill, and the trout cruise about, mouths open, drinking in their freshwater shrimp bounty. The result: Jurassic Lake's freakishly stout rainbows average 10 pounds, and regularly reach more than 20 pounds. "I'm convinced that the world-record rainbow lives somewhere in Jurassic Lake," Christer continued. "When word first started leaking about the lake, people were calling me, trying to figure out where it was. I was very cagey about its exact location. We came up with the name Jurassic Lake because of all the stones and animal skeletons around the place. It has a very prehistoric feeling." (The largest fish landed thus far weighed 28 pounds!)

All angling at Jurassic Lake is done from shore, and during the high season there's little reason to wander far from the mouth of the Barrancoso River, the one tributary that feeds into the lake; the fish gather here before spawning season. Anglers generally rely on large, subsurface patterns (Zonkers, leeches, and the like) thrown on 8-weight rods, though for the most part fly selection hardly seems to matter. "People will sometimes call and ask what colors work best, how long a wing they should tie," Christer said. "When I told them that most flies would work, they didn't seem satisfied, so now I may tell them that yellow hackle is best with a little brown on the wings—or whatever springs to mind." When the fish are coming into the stream to prepare to spawn, dry-fly fishing with more conventional trout rods can be very good, though anglers will only find "smaller" fish here, in the 5- to 10-pound class. As dusk approaches, you can wade along the shoreline and sight-fish to cruising bruisers. If you get a little buck fever casting to a dimpling 15-inch rainbow on your home stream, imagine how you'll feel dropping your Woolly Bugger in front of a pod of 15 pounders in 2 feet of water!

The chance—nay, a veritable guarantee—to catch a trout of a lifetime is a strong draw, yet Jurassic Lake may not be for everyone. For starters, there's the 230-mile, seven-and-a-half-hour drive in. Calling the road rough is an understatement; some itinerary notes suggest that anglers suffering from motion sickness or a bad back refrain from the trip. Those who've read of the startling alpine scenery of Patagonia and elegantly appointed estancias will think they've made a very wrong turn upon arrival at Jurassic. "At our first camp, we had a porcelain toilet on the rim above the lake," Christer recalled. "It was the only white object for hundreds of miles; from the seat, all you could see was pampas, which more or less resembles tundra." Your accommodations will not feature wide-screen televisions or white linen tablecloths, though the dome tents will protect you from the wind and are equipped with comfortable beds and electric lights; hot showers are also available.

By almost any estimation, the rainbow fishing at Jurassic Lake could be described as "to die for." During one visit to the camp, Christer thought that the fish had literally killed a guest. "This guy had been fishing all morning not far from the mouth of the river, and he'd landed something like fifty fish. I looked over at one point, and he was facedown in the sand. His rod hand was shaking—he had a fish on, but he had fainted. The fish had won. We carried him to his tent, and he rested. Two hours later, he was out again."

CHRISTER SJÖBERG cofounded Loop Tackle in 1979 with a simple goal: to make a living doing what he loved. Since that time, he's helped the company become a leading provider of fly tackle, especially in the growing realm of spey casting. In 1990, he helped pioneer the exploration of the Atlantic salmon rivers of the southern White Sea coast of Russia and established lodges on the Umba, Kharlovka, Litza, and Yokanga. Since that time, he's helped develop new travel programs in Patagonia.

If You Go

▶ **Prime Time:** The season is open November through mid-April; other than the period from mid-January through February, Jurassic Lake fishes fantastically—fifty- to one-hundred-fish days with fish averaging more than 10 pounds are a real possibility in the Loop River Camp during high season.

▶ **Getting There:** Anglers reach Jurassic Lake by flying into Calafate, which has service from Buenos Aires on Aerolineas Argentina (800-333-0276; www.aerolineas.com.ar).

▶ **Accommodations/Outfitters:** The best location on the lake, at the inflow of Jurassic's one tributary, is a camp operated by Loop Adventures (800-410-3133; www.loopadven tures.com). Estancia Laguna Verde (888-FISH ARGENTINA; www.estancialagunaverde .com) also operates near the lake.

▶ **Equipment:** You can opt for an 8- or 9-weight single-handed rod or a spey rod for 7- to 9-weight line; bring floating line and type 3/6 tips. You'll want at least 200 yards of backing. (A lighter 5- or 6-weight outfit is perfect for fishing the stream.) In Christer's opinion, just about any fly will work!

GULF OF CARPENTARIA

RECOMMENDED BY **Greg Bethune**

At the northernmost tip of the continent of Australia—across the Torres Strait from Papua New Guinea—anglers will find the most robust, varied, and uncrowded saltwater fly fishery they've probably never heard of: Cape York and the Gulf of Carpentaria. "There are three things that make the western edge of the Cape York Peninsula a very special place for fly fishers," Captain Greg Bethune opined. "First, there are no other anglers where we fish. No other people. Not a building, not a boat. I had one American angler tell me as we traveled down the coast on our mother ship—'I can accept that the fishing will be as good as I have heard, but I can't believe that there isn't going to be anyone else. . . . If the fishing is good, it's got to be crowded.' As we traveled down the coast only 2 miles offshore, I could see the continued amazement on his face as we put the miles behind us and all we saw were miles of deserted beaches, river mouths, and flats. Another important facet of the cape is that the wind is *always* at your back. Trade winds blow from the east and south most of the year. Since Cape York faces the north, its west coast is protected. No matter how hard the wind blows, it's always calm close to the shore and on the flats and in the rivers.

"Tremendous species variety is the perhaps the greatest attraction of Cape York for me. There are more than sixty species available to catch; fly anglers who like to count species have recorded more than thirty different species in the course of a week. You can chase high-speed pelagics like tuna and mackerel close inshore, dredge with sinking lines over the rubble reefs for a multitude of reef species like coral trout, or sight-fish on the river mouth flats for trevally, queenfish, giant herring (up to 10 pounds), and the famed Indo-Pacific permit. The brackish sections of the lower rivers are home to barramundi, mangrove snappers; 5-odd miles upstream the rivers become fresh, and you'll find exotic

OPPOSITE:

The last cast of the day at the mouth of Doughboy River, one of the Tropic Paradise*'s many stops in the Gulf of Carpentaria.*

33

species like saratoga and coal grunters that are eager to take top water flies. I don't know of any other place in the world where you can catch a blue-water tuna on the fly in the morning, a saltwater barramundi by midday, and a sweet water saratoga in the afternoon."

The fly-fishing tour de force of western Cape York unfolds over 100 miles of coastline that includes eleven rivers and river flats. Your home for the expedition is the *Tropic Paradise*, a 62-foot ship designed specifically for conveying anglers up and down these fishing grounds. It's essentially a floating fishing lodge. (Fishing is conducted from smaller skiffs that are stored on the mother ship.) The boat will motor to its southern terminus, and then slowly make its way north, stopping at regular intervals to fish. "I've been fishing these waters for twenty years, and there are still spots I haven't fished," Greg added. He went on to describe an average day. "Anglers can choose what they want to pursue after breakfast, but generally we'll fish the deeper water out in front of our mooring to beat up on some tuna and mackerel species or fish the rubble reefs before there's any wind. We don't need to go more than 3 miles off the beach to find pelagics.

"When the sun gets up a bit and if the tides are moving onto the river mouth flats and beaches, we'll do some sight-fishing for queenfish, trevally, or permit. After a chef-prepared lunch on the boat, we may head inshore to fish one of the rivers. If the tide is right, the afternoon can be a great time to target queenies.

"If I were ever restricted to catching only one species here, it would be queenfish. When they are on, they are generally schooled up and you never just catch one or two, you catch them until your hands are cut and burned and your shoulders and arms ache. They readily take any offering—especially and more spectacularly surface poppers—and they jump a lot. When the queenies are on, all of our skiffs will be in sight of each other, with the guides stirring the fish up with hookless poppers, trying to get them to splash anglers in other boats. We'll also play games, seeing if an angler can make a cast and retrieve *without* hooking a fish, or see how long you can have a queenie on with the hook bent round and the point touching the shank. On many occasions, I've seen an angler hook up and have a big queenie pull off 100 yards of backing and throw the hook, only to have another fish grab the fly as he reels the backing in and take off another 100 yards."

A species of great curiosity for western anglers is the snub-nosed dart—recently rebranded as the Indo-Pacific permit. These fish (*Trachinotus blochii*) closely resemble and are closely related to their better known Caribbean counterpart (*Trachinotus falcatus*), and display a similarly finicky nature . . . which makes them one of the Gulf of Carpentaria's great prizes. "Permit is permit is permit the world over," Greg said. "I have seen good anglers humbled by this animal with a brain the size of a pea. We have them in numbers, and we have them wired. If you have the casting skill and patience, you can add Indo-Pacific permit to your life list of species. Hooking one is just the start; anglers who have caught both (including yours truly) reckon that, pound for pound, Indo-Pacific permit pull the Atlantic permit backward. They are a hard fish to hook and even harder to land, with your heart in your mouth the whole time."

The wild beauty of the Cape York coastline—an idyllic place, despite the malevolent presence of saltwater crocodiles—has the potential to arouse amorous passion as well as piscine passion . . . and sometimes both simultaneously, as Greg shared. "I had an American visitor who was very passionate about catching Indo-Pacific permit. He was actually the first American fly angler to catch one in Australia. His wife had been pestering him for four days to take her to a deserted beach for a little—uh, shell collecting—but he kept dodging her. On the fifth day he consented, and they went to the beach. Satisfied with their excursion, they returned to the skiff. En route to the mother ship, the husband saw a pair of big permit coming down the beach in two feet of water. He grabbed his rod, made a cast, and connected. His wife is not an angler, but she dutifully helped land the fish, his fifth of the trip, and all was wonderful. The husband shared this story with another guest, who happened to be an editor for one of Australia's major papers . . . and the story, including the romantic activity on the beach, was printed.

"The week after this newspaper story ran, we had women calling, asking 'Can we do this, is it safe with the crocodiles?' My joking reply to some of these calls was 'Yes, of course it's safe. We can even offer the beach service in addition to the fishing if you'd like.'"

GREG BETHUNE was born and raised in Cairns, North Queensland, Australia. The son of a fisherman, he quickly caught the passion and was fishing on his own in local creeks by age six. After a short stint with a stock and station agency punching cows and selling agricultural chemicals, Greg was off to the Gulf of Carpentaria, where there was a developing shrimp fishery. He quickly realized there was only one job to have on a prawn trawler and that was the one in the air-conditioned wheelhouse, as the captain. Soon he became the youngest shrimper captain in the Gulf at age twenty-one. After various commercial fishing ventures for the next decade, his sport-fishing passion took over, and he bought his first charter boat and proceeded to pioneer the Cape York inshore sport and fly fishery. Greg designed and purpose-built his current 63-foot mothership, *Tropic Paradise*, in 2002 and is constantly developing new fisheries around the Cape York wilderness.

If You Go

▶ **Prime Time:** The fishing season goes year-round, though the best months for permit are May through December.

▶ **Getting There:** Visitors will first have to reach Cairns, which is served by many international carriers. From Cairns, you'll fly to Cape York via Skytrans (+61 1300 759 872; www.skytrans.com.au). After an overnight in Cape York, you can board the *Tropic Paradise* to begin your adventure.

▶ **Accommodations/Outfitter:** Carpentaria Seafaris (+61 0740 916 688; www.seafaris .com) is the Cape York region's main outfitter, leading one-week trips aboard the 62-foot *Tropic Paradise*.

▶ **Equipment:** You'll utilize several rods off Cape York. Bring 9-weights outfitted with intermediate clear lines and 10-weights with sinking shooting heads. Reels should be outfitted with at least 200 yards of Dacron backing and a strong disc drag system. Flies should include Clousers in a variety of colors, Surf Candys, Poppers, and Merkin crabs in size 1/0, 2/0, and 3/0.

CENTRAL HIGHLANDS

RECOMMENDED BY **Ken Orr**

Among eighteen-hour, halfway-around-the-world trout fishing destinations, the South Island of New Zealand has grabbed much of the limelight. But another thousand miles west (if you are traveling from North America) rests another island that beckons anglers eager to sight-fish healthy-size wild browns and rainbows in an environment that at first seems familiar, but on closer inspection appears almost otherworldly.

That island would be Tasmania.

"The history of trout in Tasmania goes back to 1864, when brown trout eggs were brought here from England," Ken Orr explained. "The intent of the original settlers was to introduce salmon—they brought 100,000 Atlantic salmon eggs, and just 4,000 trout eggs. Once the salmon fry hatched, they went to sea never to be seen again. The trout, however, found a perfect environment to live and breed. We fish for the progeny of those fish today. These fish have never been impacted by disease, and have no predators beyond man. John Randolph [of *Fly Fisherman* magazine] has called our fish perhaps the purest strain of brown trout extant. Many may not realize that New Zealand's brown trout came from our brown trout stock. Our rainbows came from California's Russian River at the turn of the century. I've heard that eggs from our rainbows have been harvested and sent back to California so Golden State rainbow stocks can be replenished with an endemic strain of fish."

The Australian state of Tasmania rests some 150 miles south across the Bass Strait from Melbourne; it's sometimes called "the island off the island." It's Australia but not the warm and dry Australia overseas visitors imagine from tour brochures; in fact, its climate might be likened more to that of the South Island of New Zealand! Although its highest peak is just above 5,000 feet, Tasmania is considered the most mountainous

island of its size (one-third larger than Switzerland) in the world. Thirty-five percent of the island is protected by world heritage and national park status. Tasmania boasts some of the best-preserved temperate forests left in the world, mixed with wild alpine moors, grand mountain scenery, and pristine streams, tarns, and lakes, all of which seem to hold trout. "You could be fishing within a half hour of getting off a plane in Launceston or Hobart," Ken continued. "Just stop and buy a license and drop a fly in the first creek or stream you come across—there will be a half-pound trout waiting. Travel a bit further to the Central Highlands region, and you'll have a chance to cast to browns that will push 6 pounds."

Where visitors to the South Island hike clear rivers (sometimes many miles) to find isolated feeding fish, Tassie anglers do a majority of their angling on smallish still waters—tiny tarns (glacially formed ponds, sometimes less than an acre in size) and lagoons (shallow, weedy lakes with wadable shallows around the margins). "We predominately sight-fish," Ken said, "stalking likely waters, presenting to individual fish. Sometimes we'll see rising trout, other times we'll spot fish cruising; we call it 'polaroiding.' At low-light times, we'll look for browns in very shallow water, just 3 to 4 inches deep. Their dorsal fins are out of the water. It's like hunting bonefish on a saltwater flat. We even call the fish 'tailers.'"

Over more than thirty years of guiding, Orr has noticed that many of his clients have a learning curve they must climb to find success on Tassie tarns and lagoons. "I've found that the average American angler is not a quick caster, or necessarily an accurate caster," he offered. "The way we're fishing, you need to present both quickly and accurately—if we can see the fish, the fish can see us, and there's no time for ten false casts. Long casts are seldom necessary, however. When the browns are up in the shallows, we'll fish to them with small nymphs tied 3 or 4 inches below a bushy dry fly; a popular setup might be a Stick Caddis on the dropper, with a Red Tag [a beetle pattern] on top. When you see fish that are cruising, you present the fly far enough ahead so you don't spook them, yet close enough so they don't change direction—3 feet ahead is often about right. When the fish sees the fly, they accelerate, and you'll see the action. The takes on the nymph are usually very gentle. The dry fly just skitters on the water. In the excitement, anglers will tend to preempt their strike. It's adrenaline-pumping stuff. As the angler is preparing to make the cast and set the hook, you can hear the line shaking in the rod. Most come away saying that they've never experienced this style of fishing before."

OPPOSITE: Much of Tasmania's best brown-trout angling involves sight fishing on small lakes or tarns.

Though angling is a popular pastime in Tasmania, crowds are seldom a problem. "In the Western Lakes region alone, there are some three thousand tarns and lagoons that all contain wild trout," Ken continued. "Where I like to go on a given day is very weather dependent. If it's going to be too cold for good feeding activity on the higher elevation lakes, we'll drop down to lower level lakes, or fish a stream. In the still waters, the fish generally range from 1 to 2.5 pounds, but they fight exceptionally hard; most take you into your backing. Our browns jump like rainbows and will try to bury you in the weeds. They really seem to be thinking; sometimes when they're hooked, you'll see them turn on the side where the fly is and rub that side along the bottom, trying to scrape the hook off."

Two of Tasmania's best-known lagoons are Penstock and Little Pine. "Penstock has huge weed beds, which sustain a tremendous food chain. There are good mayfly populations, and later in the season, you'll have gum beetles, flying ants, and hoppers on the water. On a good day at Penstock, you might expect to be broken off several times, and to get a 5- or 6-pound brown to hand. Little Pine may be Tasmania's most famous dry-fly fishery, with huge mayfly hatches."

If Orr were to offer a final bit of advice for Tassie anglers, it would be to ignore the fish—at least on occasion. "We encourage visitors to open themselves up to a total Tasmania experience. Much of our flora is endemic, not found anywhere else in the world. The same can be said of our animals. Every day we see wildlife—wallabies, kangaroos, quolls, spiny anteater, platypus. You might encounter a Tasmanian devil wandering up a stream bank." (Yes, there really is a basis for the Looney Tunes cartoon character; devils are carnivorous marsupials the size of a smallish dog that pose no danger to humans.)

"At the end of a week of fishing, I hope people remember the experience as much as the trout."

KEN ORR is a third-generation fly fisher and the son of a well-known and respected fly angler and nymph specialist, the late Jack Orr. At the age of eight, he was presented with his first cane fly rod and silk line and faced the early frustrations of learning to fly fish. He was totally hooked and could think of little else other than his next tutorial weekend on dry fly or nymph. In 1978, with the assistance of good friend and Tasmania's first guide, Noel Jetson, he established his own trout guiding business, Ken Orr's Tasmanian Trout Expeditions. For more than forty years of fly fishing he has been fortunate to represent Australia on many occasions at international fly-fishing competitions. Ken is honored to have fished with and count as friends famed international anglers such as Gary and Jason Borger, Jack Dennis, the late Gary Lafontaine, Mike Lawson, and Doug Swisher. He is a Federation of Fly Fishers Certified Casting Instructor. Over the years, he has produced many magazine articles and product reviews and was a contributor to the book *Australia's Best Trout Flies*. He has become a Trout Fishing Ambassador for the Tasmanian Department of Tourism running fly-fishing seminars, attending shows, and fishing throughout Australia, New Zealand, Japan, Canada, and the United States. He has been the guest angler on many national and international TV shows and films promoting Tasmania and its wild brown trout fishery.

If You Go

▶ **Prime Time:** The trout season is open from August through April. Hatches occur more regularly during the Aussie summer (January through March).

▶ **Getting There:** Most visitors reach Tasmania via Sydney or Melbourne. Service is offered to both Launceston and Hobart by Qantas Airways (800-227-4500; www.qantas .com).

▶ **Accommodations:** Angling Retreats (+61 3 6289 1191; www.orrsometassietrout.com .au) is centrally located and caters to anglers. Other lodging options are listed at www .discovertasmania.com.

▶ **Guides/Outfitters:** There are a number of guides that lead anglers to Tasmania's trout, including Ken Orr (+61 3 6289 1191; www.orrsometassietrout.com.au) and Peter Hayes (+61 3 6397 5073; www.flyfishtasmania.com.au).

▶ **Equipment:** If you were to bring only one rod, Ken suggests a 6-weight outfitted with floating line, as this will allow you to contend with wind; smaller outfits will suffice on calm days and for streams. A sink tip or intermediate line is helpful for early season fishing. Guides are happy to provide flies, though many common American patterns (Royal Wulff, Adams, beadhead nymphs) do well.

PUNTA GORDA

RECOMMENDED BY **Jim Klug**

Some great fly-fishing destinations *are* great because of the tremendous diversity they offer. Think southwest Alaska for species diversity (leopard rainbows, five salmon species, and char) or Yellowstone for habitat diversity (small streams, large rivers, lakes). Others are considered great thanks to the singular focus of their respective angling offerings. Homosassa Springs will be forever equated with tarpon, New Brunswick's Miramichi with Atlantic salmon. For those in the know, Punta Gorda, near Belize's southern border with Guatemala and Honduras, means permit.

"Punta Gorda has largely escaped the attention that many top flats destinations around the Caribbean have received," Jim Klug said. "While not completely unknown, it does not receive the amount of pressure that other places see. Why? Because Punta Gorda is for anglers that want to focus on permit. It doesn't consistently deliver the diversity that many anglers are looking for. Some anglers *think* they want to focus on permit until their third fishless day. Then a voice inside says 'How about a bonefish?' The late Jack Samson, a well-known permit addict (and author of *Fly Fishing for Permit* and *Permit on a Fly*) once told me, 'To be a good permit fisherman, you have to not mind *not* catching fish.'"

For fly anglers, permit are considered the holy grail among the light tackle sport fish of the Caribbean. Their broad body, large round eyes, blunt face, and a black sickle-shaped tail make them unmistakable. Permit's aerodynamics give them tremendous strength; specimens, which can run from 5 to 40 pounds and above, have been known to rip 150 yards of line out in their first run. Secretive, antsy, and ever alert, permit are the spookiest creatures on the saltwater flats. To catch a permit on a fly, you have to do a lot of things right—cast a large fly 40 or 50 feet, often into whipping winds, mimic the halting gait of a crab with your retrieve, and play a very strong animal on light line around

OPPOSITE:
There's only one
reason anglers
go to Punta
Gorda—permit!

43

coral heads that wait to part you from your prize. For a long time, flats cognoscenti did not believe that permit could be regularly caught with a fly. That perception changed in the early eighties, when several Florida Keys anglers—guide Steve Huff and Del Brown among them—began building flies with epoxy to imitate the small crabs that are a staple of the permit's diet. With the evolution of crab patterns—Del's Merkin, Mathew's Turneffe Crab, and the Rag Head among them—odds for enticing permit to strike have increased.

"I first fished for permit in the early nineties, in the Yucatán and Bahamas," Jim continued. "The more I fished them, the more I began researching other permit areas. All the arrows pointed to southern Belize. At that time, there were only a handful of people fishing permit with any regularity around Punta Gorda. On my first trip down, I fished with a young guy named Scully Garbutt. He was new to the guide scene and still figuring out the fly-fishing thing at that time. At that point, he only had a handful of trips under his belt. The first morning out, we hooked four fish and landed three. Even at a young age, he was one of the fishiest guides I had ever met. Today he's considered one of the best permit guides in the world." Scully, along with his brothers, Oliver and Eworth, is the core of Punta Gorda's guide force. The Garbutts, along with older brother, Dennis (who manages operations), run Garbutt Brothers Lodge, the resting place of choice for anglers in this once quiet fishing town that's slowly discovering the possibilities of ecotourism. (Bird and manatee watching, jungle tours, snorkeling, and nearby Mayan ruins all attract visitors.) "This small lodge is not a fancy, over-the-top kind of place," Jim added, "but it has a great location overlooking Joe Taylor Creek and the Caribbean. It's clean, it's air-conditioned, and there's freshly cooked food with a Creole flavor and cold Belikin beer at the lodge's Grand Slam Bar. It's a base of operations for fishermen, built by fishermen. You're often out on the water for ten to twelve hours a day, so you don't need a lot more." The lodge is in Punta Gorda proper, so if you're looking for a taste of southern Belize life, it's only a stroll or bike ride away.

For those seeking permit, however, the search unfolds around a seemingly endless series of pancake flats. "All throughout this area of southern Belize there are hundreds of these flats that rise out of blue water," Jim continued. "Some might be half a football field long, others might be the size of a small parking lot. In the course of a day, you'll probably hopscotch your way around to several dozens of these flats. It's all classic style, quintessential permit fishing. Most fish are found on the shallow flats, and there's very little fishing that takes place in deeper waters. Oftentimes the guide will drift up on to one of the flats; if he sees fish tailing, you'll get out of the boat and approach the fish on foot. If not, he might pole around the edge. You might find small groups of two or three fish at a time or schools of several dozen fish. You'll need long leaders, a variety of crab patterns, and you'll have to drop the fly into the permit's feeding zone—to the front of the fish, not 10 feet away, but right on their beak. You just hope that they don't blow up when it drops.

"It's not the easiest kind of fishing, and it doesn't necessarily result in the biggest numbers. But it's permit fishing as it was meant to be."

Put another way: The angler who lands a permit on the pancake flats off Punta Gorda really deserves that cold Belikin at the end of the day!

JIM KLUG is the founder, co-owner, and director of operations for Yellow Dog Flyfishing Adventures, which orchestrates fly-fishing trips all over the world. Jim has worked in the fly-fishing industry as a guide, sales rep, travel coordinator, and as past national sales manager for Scientific Anglers. He has guided extensively throughout the western United States, and has fished in more than twenty-five countries around the world. Jim spends a lot of time in the Caribbean, South America, and Alaska, working with Yellow Dog's network of lodges and guides. Jim is also the co-owner and the executive producer for Confluence Films, the makers of *DRIFT* and *RISE*. His writings and photographs have appeared in numerous magazines and other publications.

If You Go

▶ **Prime Time:** Permit are present around Punta Gorda throughout the year.

▶ **Getting There:** First fly to Belize City via American Airlines (800-433-7300; www.aa.com), Continental Airlines (800-523-3273; www.continental.com), or US Airways (800-428-4322; www.usairways.com). Regular flights to Punta Gorda are available from Maya Island Air (501-223-1140; www.mayaregional.com) and Tropic Air (800-422-3435; www.tropicair.com).

▶ **Accommodations/Guides:** Most anglers stay with the Garbutts. Booking is through Yellow Dog Flyfishing Adventures (888-777-5060; www.yellowdogflyfishing.com).

▶ **Equipment:** A 9-weight rod with floating line and at least 200 yards of 20-pound backing will ready you for Punta Gorda. Yellow Dog can provide a list of popular flies.

TURNEFFE ATOLL

RECOMMENDED BY **Steve Abel**

"I've fished all over the Caribbean," Steve Abel began, "and there are several things that make Turneffe Atoll in Belize stand out from most other locations. First, you're on your own island. It's just you, a handful of other guests, and the employees. Taking the boat out to Turneffe from the mainland adds to your sense of adventure and feeling of really getting away. Second, the guides all speak excellent English. That's not to say that guides in other places aren't very good, but the language barrier can be difficult to overcome, especially for a beginner. The same guides have been there for years. Most importantly, at Turneffe, you have a very legitimate chance at a grand slam. There are lots of permit around, bonefish are extremely plentiful, and tarpon are also present—especially from May to August, when the migratory fish show up. As you move east in the Caribbean, bonefish often become your lone option. I like the diversity that Turneffe offers."

Turneffe Atoll is 30 miles east of Belize City. It's the largest of Belize's three coral atolls at nearly 300 square miles and boasts approximately 450 islands and some 400 small ponds and lagoons. Turneffe Flats Lodge, the home for most anglers visiting the atoll, rests a few hundred yards from the coral lip that separates the atoll. "The flats right in front of the lodge have excellent fishing," Steve continued. "You can step out of your bungalow, and see tailing bonefish from the deck. Ten steps later, you're on the flats, getting ready to cast. Permit also come in on the tides. If you have a non-angler with you, they don't have to sit on the beach the whole time you're fishing. The lodge has an adventure program where a guide will take a group out snorkeling or to find dolphins or even to search for saltwater crocodiles. The snorkeling is unbelievable. I always set aside an hour for snorkeling after the day's fishing is done. Sometimes I'll go with a fly rod in my hand and catch barracuda while trolling a fly as I swim along."

OPPOSITE:
Brian O'Keefe
lines up a
bonefish not
far from the
eastern edge of
Turneffe Atoll.

Barring inclement weather, the visiting angler is nearly certain to have many shots at permit while poling around Turneffe . . . though whether the fish grab or not is, of course, another matter! The deep waters surrounding Turneffe shelter robust permit populations, and its pristine lagoons provide ideal feeding habitat for the fish, which enter the lagoons during rising tides. Turneffe's Central Lagoon—some 15 miles in length—attracts many fish, sometimes in sizable schools. The routine for targeting fish here is somewhat different than at other permit locales: guides slowly motor 40 or 50 yards off the mangroves, scanning for nervous water or the hint of a black dorsal fin extending above the blue-green waters. (This allows anglers to cover a great amount of water, increasing the odds of locating fish.) "Once you find cruising fish," Steve continued, "you throw a crab pattern ahead of them, and strip it when the fish get close." The permit at Turneffe have apparently missed the articles about their species' skittishness. Anglers have reported casting repeatedly into large schools, beginning at the edges and moving their offerings to the center of the group. The fish did not take, but they did not scatter, either.

If you're fortunate enough to pick up a permit, it should not be difficult to find a bonefish for the second check mark on your grand slam scorecard. Much of Turneffe's bonefishing occurs on flats adjoining the coral reefs on the eastern edge of the island. As the tide comes in, it's often possible to watch the fish queue up at the edge of the flats to come up and feed; this can make for easy pickings. "I recall a visit to Turneffe a few years back," Steve said. "There's a flat that's just north of the lodge, across a cut. It's probably the most fished flat around, thanks to its proximity to the lodge. As we motored toward the flat that morning, a boat was already there. We continued north. We decided to go back to the lodge for lunch, and we passed the flat again. The guys that were there earlier were still there. As we were having lunch, the two anglers from the flat—both elderly gentlemen— came in. 'How did you do?' I asked. The first angler said, 'Well, I caught thirty-five bonefish. And I'm blind. My buddy caught twenty-five fish.' 'How did you do it?' I asked. 'The guide would point my rod and say "35 feet" or "45 feet." Then I'd make the cast.' The blind fisherman was eighty-five years old; his friend was seventy-six!" While not huge, the bonefish at Turneffe are good size by Belizean standards, averaging between 3 and 6 pounds; 10-pound specimens are encountered with some regularity.

With two-thirds of your grand slam covered, you'll now need to find a tarpon. This is not a particularly difficult task in the summer months (as mentioned earlier), but even in the winter, it's quite possible. "There are tarpon present year-round at Turneffe," Steve added. "You can generally dredge up a fish—sometimes a large one—from one of the deep cuts. Smaller fish can be found in some of the little ponds; the guides know where they are if you need a tarpon to get your grand slam."

STEVE ABEL, master machinist and creative metallurgical technician, was born in Oceanside, California, and grew up fishing the area's beaches and piers. His family moved north to Ventura County when he was about ten, which set him off in search of trout in Sespe Creek, Piru Creek, and other streams that drained into the Pacific. Steve worked as a salvage diver in the Suez Canal following the Six-Day War and in various machine shops where he honed his skills. In the mid-1970s, he and three brothers opened their own small machine shop, turning out precision screws and parts for everything from aluminum screen doors to aerospace and pacemaker parts. With success in the shop, his love of fishing and friends prompted him to build some prototype fly reels in the mid-1980s; and in 1987 he researched, developed, and tested what was to evolve into the Abel Reel. That reel was introduced to the public in January 1988. After years of eighteen-hour days and all the tribulations of forty employees, plus a battle with mouth cancer, he and his wife, Gina, sold Abel Reels to an investment group. Today, Steve fishes, hunts, and spends as much time as possible on Montana's Bitterroot River.

If You Go

▶ **Prime Time:** Bonefish and permit are present at Turneffe throughout the year; adult migratory tarpon are reliably present in the summer months.

▶ **Getting There:** Turneffe Atoll is reached via Belize City, which is served by American Airlines (800-433-7300; www.aa.com), Continental Airlines (800-523-3273; www.continental.com), and US Airways (800-428-4322; www.usairways.com).

▶ **Accommodations/Guides:** Turneffe Flats Lodge (888-512-8812; www.tflats.com) is highly regarded. Most anglers visit Saturday to Saturday.

▶ **Equipment:** For bonefish: an 8-weight rod with floating line and at least 150 yards of 20-pound backing. For permit: a 9-weight rod with floating line and at least 200 yards of 20-pound backing. For tarpon: an 11- or 12-weight rod with intermediate sinking line and at least 200 yards of 30-pound backing, plus shock tippets.

ASUNTA AND PLUMA RIVERS

RECOMMENDED BY **Brian Gies**

"A few years back, I made the long trek to Tierra del Fuego to fish for sea-run brown trout on the Irigoyen River with an outfit called Far End Rivers," Brian Gies began. "I was part of the fifth group down to fish at this newly established lodge on a very exciting fishery, and one of the owners, Marcelo Perez, was showing me the property and the river. Before we'd even finished the tour of Far End Rivers, Marcel took out his laptop. 'We're very excited about this fishery in Bolivia,' he said, and began taking me through a slide show highlighting a beautiful mountain river where anglers could sight-fish to golden dorado."

A dozen years ago, few people outside of South America had heard of golden dorado, let alone knew of their potential as a fly-rod target. Native to southern Brazil, parts of Bolivia, Paraguay and Uruguay, and northeastern Argentina, golden dorado have the shape of a salmon, the jaws of a crocodile, and scales of yellow, orange, and black that radiate the fish's namesake golden sheen. Fish were said to reach weights of near 100 pounds in some of the larger river systems. The golden dorado's bellicose temperament, epic strength, and otherworldly beauty quickly catapulted them into the fly fisher's pantheon of must-fish-for species. The first venues for fly anglers seeking golden dorado comprised marshy areas of larger river systems and the rivers themselves. "There was a lot of blind casting to likely holding water," Brian continued, "and the fish in many systems were not terribly large—many in the 6- to 7-pound range, perhaps up to 15 pounds. The place that Marcelo described in Bolivia had larger fish—averaging 10 pounds, with good potential for fish of 30 pounds. Plus, the rivers were small, with clear water. As Marcelo went through the photos, I thought that if this place was only half of what they're saying it is, it will be incredible. Even though I was down in Argentina at this great new lodge to fish for sea-run browns, I found myself thinking about Bolivia."

OPPOSITE:
Some have
equated the
Bolivian
golden dorado
experience
with fishing
western Montana
streams—for
tarpon!

Fishing takes place on two remote rivers (the Asunta and Pluma) in the Isiboro-Secure National Park and Indian Reservation, a transitional zone where the Andes meet the upper Amazon. Brian described the rivers as "jungle freestones. In places, they're reminiscent of coastal steelhead streams in the Pacific Northwest or the trout streams of New Zealand's South Island. The habitat shifts dramatically, depending where you are on the river. In places, you feel like you're in the Amazon, in others like you're on braid on a river system in Alaska. The birding is off the charts, and at times you'll be overwhelmed by butterflies; a few times, we came upon a whole beach covered with butterflies. You'll often hear monkeys in the canopy, and sometimes you'll catch a glimpse. I saw jaguar tracks frequently though I never set eyes on a cat itself."

A trip to Tsimane Lodge (which has exclusive rights to fish the Asunta and Pluma, more than 50 miles of pristine river) has all the elements of an unforgettable adventure—and *adventure* is the word. After an overnight in the city of Santa Cruz, Bolivia, guests (a maximum of six) assemble at a small charter airport for a two-hour flight into the jungle. The plane delivers the guests to the Asunta Lodge and then after four nights and three days of fishing, they take a boat downstream to the Pluma Lodge for three more days of angling. "When the plane drops down to the airstrip, half of the local village—indigenous Chimán people—comes out to meet you," Brian described. "You'll also see the Chimán along the river as you boat into the second lodge—young boys shooting baitfish in the shallows with bow and arrow. It's quite a cultural experience. Marcelo is able to attract up-and-coming chefs to the lodges," Brian added, "and the food is exquisite. Breakfast is cooked to order, dinners are evocative of estancia dinners in Patagonia. One night it might be filet mignon, another wild mushroom risotto. The bar is stocked with fine Argentine wines, as well as spirits."

Each morning, anglers set out in pairs to fish a different section of the river, accompanied by an Argentine fishing guide and a Chimán boatsman to help maneuver your canoe through the rapids. While you move up- and downriver by motorized canoe, most fishing is done by wading, and anglers wade wet, as the air and water are warm. "You fish New Zealand style, working your way upstream, spotting a run and looking for fish," Brian continued. "If you see a fish, you make a game plan, depending on how the fish is behaving. We'd typically get upstream of the fish, and then cast streamers. Sometimes you just swing the fly down and across, other times you strip it fast or strip it erratically. If the fish decide to take, there's no ambiguity—they hammer the fly! I began fishing with

30-pound wire tippet and got snapped off on my first two grabs." Some have equated the experience to fishing for baby tarpon in a western Montana trout stream.

The golden dorado in the Asunta and Pluma are not year-round residents but push upriver to feed on sabalo, a baitfish that migrates up from the Mamoré River to spawn. Schools of sabalo can be so thick that the color of the river changes to a pulsing gray. Such schools can result in an almost unheard-of freshwater phenomenon. "On more than one occasion during my visit, I'd be walking upstream," Brian related, "and I'd see some very slight ripples on the soft water at the river's edge. The soft water would get a little more nervous, and then suddenly a 20-foot circle would explode. The explosion is the result of gangs of dorado—four to twelve fish—herding sabalo into the shallows, and then crashing into the schools. Dorado are flying out of the water, sabalo are flying. If you cast anywhere near the melee, you'll hook up.

"On one occasion, I hooked a 6- or 7-pound fish in one of these groups. Before I could get it under control, it was chopped in half by a larger fish."

BRIAN GIES is a cofounder and chief financial officer of Fly Water Travel (www.flywater travel.com), a team of fly-fishing travel experts dedicated to arranging trips to the world's finest fishing destinations and lodges. He has fished in Mexico, Mongolia, India, Nepal, New Zealand, Argentina, Christmas Island—and about everywhere else in between.

If You Go

▶ **Prime Time:** May through October.

▶ **Getting There:** Your charter flight to Tsimane Lodge departs from Santa Cruz, Bolivia, which is served by American Airlines (800-433-7300; www.aa.com) and AeroSur Airlines (866-903-2885; www.aerosur.com) via Miami.

▶ **Accommodations/Guides:** Tsimane Lodge is the only outfitter operating in the Isiboro–Secure National Park and Indian Reservation. Spots are limited and can be reserved through reputable fly-fishing booking agents, including Fly Water Travel.

▶ **Equipment:** You'll need an 8-weight rod outfitted with saltwater floating line and intermediate tips (and 100 yards of 30-pound backing). Popular flies include Andinos, Puglisi Streamers, and Tarpon Snakes from size 2/0 to 4/0.

SUSTUT RIVER

RECOMMENDED BY **Ken Morrish**

Every steelhead aficionado hopes to one day make the pilgrimage to northern British Columbia to fish the fabled rivers of the Skeena system. Among the storied rivers here— the Bulkley, the Babine, the Kispiox, and Mother Skeena herself—none is more treasured than the Sustut. Ken Morrish can make a passionate case for the river that's been called "Steelhead Valhalla" (indeed, a lodge of that name rests on the river's banks).

"There are three things that make the Sustut really stand out for me. First, it's a true wilderness river that's only available to those willing or able to fly in. For all intents and purposes, this is only feasible if you're staying at one of the two small lodges on the river. As a result of its distance from civilization, the Sustut is not available to freelancers, and that makes it the least-crowded Class I steelhead river in British Columbia. Since the two lodges are under the same ownership, the runs are well divided between anglers. The water is rested, and you never have to worry about someone 'low holing' you—though there's more good water on the Sustut than anyone could hope to fish in a week.

"A second great facet of the Sustut is that your odds of losing multiple days to impaired water quality are minimal by BC standards. There are few things more disappointing than getting all the way to the Bulkley or Kispiox for a long-anticipated steelhead assault only to have the rivers blown out and unfishable.

"The third quality that makes the Sustut very special is that, in my experience, it has the highest likelihood of all the rivers of the Skeena drainage of producing a 'supertanker' steelhead—that is, a fish over 25 pounds. The Sustut doesn't have the highest catch rates among the Skeena tribs, but the fish here average 14 pounds and all are thick-bodied wild fish. If anglers average one or two fish a day, it's been a pretty successful week, though a few fortunate rods each season will have a twenty-fish week. An added bonus is that Sustut

OPPOSITE:
An angler unfurls
a spey cast on one
of the Sustut's
fabled runs.
Anglers generally
average one or
two fish a day.

steelhead can be very susceptible to a dry fly, even though the river runs colder than the other rivers in the area. I've had a 20-pound fish take a Pompadour in 36-degree water."

The Sustut has its headwaters in Sustut and Johansen Lakes in the Omineca Mountains. From here, it rambles 150 miles to its confluence with the Skeena, due north of Smithers. Beyond a few lumber camps, it's wild, untrammeled country, the domain of moose, black and grizzly bears, and gray wolves. The experience of fishing the Sustut—or at least of getting to the Sustut—has evolved over the years. "When I first visited the Sustut twenty years ago, the plane would land at a small airstrip by the Skeena, and guests would board a contraption that then Steelhead Valhalla lodge owner Dennis Farnesworth called a rail speeder," Ken recalled. "It was a rickety go-kart powered by a lawn mower engine, with plywood walls. You'd pile all your gear on, then stand in, and the rail speeder would putter up some old railroad tracks. When the tracks stopped, you'd shoulder your gear and hike the last half mile in. Today, the Caravan that brings you in lands on a gravel airstrip closer to the lodge."

The fishing program on the Sustut is well defined. After a hearty breakfast, anglers climb into a jetboat to be spirited off to the day's beat. The Sustut is divided into four primary beats, which are in turn divided into an upper and lower section. By monitoring who's fishing which beats, the lodge operators (Steelhead Valhalla and Suskeena) ensure that no section sees too much pressure and that anglers get to experience all the water that the Sustut has to offer. (The lodges can also access a run on the Skeena.) Beyond the tremendous scenery—and the chance that every cast could be swinging past steelhead in excess of 40 inches—there are several highlights to a week on the Sustut. "For me, the most dramatic day of the week is when you travel downriver to fish the main stem of the Skeena," Ken continued. "The valley opens up more down there, and some of the pools have staggering views of the snowcapped mountains, augmented with the reds and golds of the trees. I remember stepping out onto a sandbar that was entirely covered in wolf tracks, which strikes home the unspoiled nature of this wilderness setting. The days you visit the upper beat are also memorable. The jetboat has to negotiate a rock garden to reach the upper beat, and zigzagging past the boulders is like running a slalom course. At the top of the upper beat, there's a famous pool where the Bear River empties into the Sustut. It's an easy pool to fish and almost always holds big fish.

"One of my favorite pools on the upper fishable section of the Sustut is called The Aquarium. At this pool, you can often see the fish, and I love to watch my angling partner cast and see how the fish react to the fly. I used to think that steelhead responded only as the fly swung close by—say, within 8 or 10 feet. But at a pool like The Aquarium, my understanding of steelhead behavior was forever changed. Sometimes, the fish start to react when the fly is more than 40 feet above them. They seem to be able to feel when the line and fly hit the water. I've seen them track the fly from 20 feet away, coming up to the fly, nudging it, even nibbling it. There have been occasions when a guy has a tight line, and he has no idea. Sometimes they'll look at the fly on every cast.

"Watching steelhead on the upper Sustut has been very educational."

KEN MORRISH is cofounder and co-owner of Fly Water Travel, a team of fly-fishing travel experts dedicated to arranging trips to the world's finest fishing destinations and lodges. He is a fourth-generation fly fisher and has guided throughout Alaska, Oregon, and California. Ken has taught hundreds of students the fundamentals of the sport, managed fly shops, consulted with leading fly rod manufacturers, and designed an extensive line of popular fly patterns produced by Idylwilde Flies of Portland, Oregon. Ken's angling travels have taken him around the world. An accomplished writer and photographer, his work has appeared in *Patagonia, Outside, Fly Fisherman, Fly Rod & Reel, Northwest Fly Fishing, Wild Steelhead and Salmon*, and other popular publications.

If You Go

► **Prime Time:** September and October. September fish are inclined to take dry flies. October has more fish present.

► **Getting There:** Sustut adventures stage in Smithers, BC, which is served by Air Canada (888-247-2262; www.aircanada.com) via Vancouver.

► **Accommodations/Guides:** Lodges here have very limited availability and can be booked through a number of reputable booking agencies, including Fly Water Travel (800-552-2729; www.flywatertravel.com).

► **Equipment:** Most prefer spey rods for the Sustut, for 7- to 10-weight lines. Bring floating lines and sinking tips ranging from type 6 to type 14. Traditional steelhead patterns, skaters, and weighted bunny leeches will all come in handy.

COLUMBIA RIVER

RECOMMENDED BY **Geoff Mueller**

The name "Columbia River" is not synonymous with "rainbow trout." For most, the Columbia is a vast, half-mile-wide or more expanse, in a few places a raging torrent, in most as placid as a lake, thanks to the taming effect of fourteen hydroelectric dams. It's a place where anglers may pull plugs for chinook salmon in the spring and fall or drown chicken gizzards below lower dams in search of giant sturgeon. It's a waterway that steel-head (a *form* of rainbow trout) use as a superhighway en route to the Deschutes, the Grande Ronde, and the Clearwater (among other natal streams). But when you stand above the turbines at Bonneville Dam or on the ramparts of the Astoria-Megler Bridge where the river meets the Pacific, trout fishing does not enter your mind.

However, some 770 miles upriver from the Pacific, the Columbia has a slightly different face. It's still a large river, sometimes running at more than 100,000 cubic feet per second. It's still very much a tailwater, issuing forth from the Hugh Keenleyside and Brilliant Dams (which create Arrow and Kootenay Lakes, respectively) in the town of Castlegar, British Columbia. But instead of being a river that anglers gaze upon as they careen toward other waters, the Columbia that pours through the Ootischenia Valley for 30 miles above the border with Washington State is a destination unto itself, one of the greatest dry-fly fisheries in North America you may never have heard of.

"I grew up near Vancouver, BC, and I'd never fished in the eastern part of the province," Geoff Mueller began. "After I finished journalism school, I took a job at the *Castlegar News*. I spent my first summer there trying to figure out the river during my afternoons and evenings, walking and wading it. I soon realized that you really needed a boat to properly approach the river. I began hanging out at the one fly shop in town [Castlegar Sport Centre and Fly Shop] and eventually convinced the owner [Rod Zavaduk] that he should take me out on the river. Once I got a taste of what fishing the Columbia's big eddies during the caddis hatch could be like, I bought an aluminum car-topper, with a circa 1970 Johnson 10-horse—just enough boat to put me into the action."

The section of the Columbia below Castlegar rests in the heart of the West Kootenay, an area bounded by the Selkirk Mountains to the west and Kootenay Lake in the east. This region is frequently overlooked by anglers in favor of the famed steelhead waters to the north, the lakes of the Kamloops region to the west, and the Bow across the Canadian Rockies to the east. "Fly fishers in British Columbia and Alberta have known about the Columbia for some time," Geoff continued, "but it was largely under the radar for eastern Canada and the United States . . . until *Fly Fisherman* ran an article declaring it British Columbia's best dry-fly stream. Despite the ink it's received, the Columbia remains uncrowded. It's pretty out of the way, and it's not your typical trout stream."

Many of the rainbows in the West Kootenay segment of the Columbia are Gerrard strain fish. Gerrard rainbows, endemic to Trout Lake and the Lardeau River (just north of Kootenay Lake), grow to gigantic proportions, averaging five times the size of the Kamloops rainbows encountered in much of interior British Columbia. In Kootenay Lake, these fish feed primarily on kokanee salmon and can reach weights of more than 40 pounds. In the Columbia, lacking kokanees as forage, the fish don't grow quite as large, though the largest one landed still tipped the scales at a whopping 23 pounds. (Early spring brings the best odds for hooking into a double-digit rainbow on the river, by swinging big leeches on sink-tip lines along gravel bars, much like winter steelhead fishing.)

While the stretch of water between Castlegar and Trail has its wadable riffles, the best fishing generally occurs in the river's many huge eddies—mammoth buffet turntables where the main entrée for the river's resident rainbows is a potpourri of caddis, led by the Grannom (or Mother's Day) caddis. On the Columbia, the little encrusted casings you might inspect while wading are well below your feet—as much as 50 or 60 feet below— hence the need for a boat. The eddies collect massive amounts of insect life, and the rainbows key in. A given eddy—Waterloo and Kootenay are popular ones—may have a hundred fish finning in the current, snouts in the air, feeding to their stomach's content, and occasionally dropping down into the vortex to rest and digest. As night falls, the feeding reaches a frenzied pace, with scores of fish slurping in casting distance—an exciting, but disconcerting prospect for many. Most of the fish are at least 16 inches; each eddy will have a number of fish on the north side of 20 inches. "With tremendous numbers of fish feeding, it's tempting to tie on an elk-hair Caddis and start casting into the melee," Geoff said. "You're much better off observing the feeding lanes that the fish are working so you can get a sense of the rhythm of individual trout's feeding pattern—and whether they're taking adults or emergers. You have a lot of competition for your fly; getting in sync with the fish will result in more hook-ups.

"There's some very good stillwater fishing in the area (among these options are Lower Arrow and Kootenay Lakes) and small stream angling as well," Geoff added. If you've come this far, you might head a few hours east to take in some of eastern British Columbia's other little-known dry-fly gems—the Slocan, the St. Mary, and the Elk.

GEOFF MUELLER is senior editor at *The Drake*. He cut his editorial teeth working the interior BC newspaper circuit. Before joining *The Drake*, he was managing editor at *Fly Fisherman* magazine and is a frequent contributor at *Angling Trade* and BC-based *Kootenay Mountain Culture* magazines. Geoff has chased trout across the continent, but has recently fallen hard for beachscapes and salty prey.

If You Go

▶ **Prime Time:** The Columbia's prolific caddis hatches begin in earnest in June and continue through summer into the early fall.

▶ **Getting There:** Castlegar has service from Vancouver and Calgary on Air Canada (888-247-2262; www.aircanada.com). It's roughly a three-hour drive from Spokane, which is served by many airlines, including Alaska Airlines (800-252-7522; www.alaskaair.com).

▶ **Accommodations:** The town of Castlegar (www.castlegar.com) offers a range of lodging options. The nearby resort towns of Nelson (www.discovernelson.com) and Rossland (www.rossland.com) provide more upscale lodging.

▶ **Guides/Outfitters:** Several outfitters lead float trips on the Columbia, including Castlegar Sport Centre and Fly Shop (250-365-8288; www.castlegarflyshop.ca) and Dave Brown Outfitters (800-453-3991; www.davebrownoutfitters.com).

▶ **Equipment:** A 5- or 6-weight rod outfitted with floating line will be well matched for the Columbia. The Castlegar Fly Shop will have a good idea of what caddis imitations are working at the time of your visit.

SAN DIEGO

RECOMMENDED BY **Conway Bowman**

The phrase "fly fishing for sharks" has a rhetorical flourish to it that's ungrounded in reality, like "shooting arrows at the sun" or "shadowboxing the apocalypse." For Conway Bowman, it's just another day on the waters around San Diego's Mission Bay.

"I grew up in the San Diego area," Conway began, "and my first fly-fishing experiences were up on Silver Creek in Idaho, casting to trout during the summer. During the winters back home, I would go bass fishing in local lakes, but there were not many other freshwater opportunities. In the early nineties, I discovered saltwater fly fishing and soon learned that sharks were among the most plentiful sport fish off the coast of southern California. I bought a 17-foot aluminum boat and began pursuing them. After catching twenty-five blue sharks on my first day out, I realized I was on to something. It took me two years longer to figure out how to get mako sharks to take the fly. Nowadays, if I can draw a mako into the chum slick near the boat, there's almost a 100 percent chance that we'll hook it." In 2009, on Conway's best day, his boat hooked twenty-three makos, landing and releasing fifteen, with some fish more than 200 pounds.

Shortfin mako sharks are found throughout much of the world, including the waters of the Pacific immediately off the coast of San Diego. "This area is one of three breeding areas for shortfins," Conway explained. "They're generally blue-water fish, but the Continental Shelf pinches in close to the beach here. Once they're born, there's a good deal of forage [primarily bonito and tuna] for them within a few miles of shore. Most of the fish we chase are juveniles—that is, under 300 pounds. They're here from May through August. In recent years, it seems that we're finding the fish closer and closer to shore. We hooked one fish last year less than a quarter mile off the beach. I could see my wife's car parked by the beach as the fish was jumping."

61

Mature makos can reach more than 12 feet in length and weights exceeding 1,200 pounds, and are considered the fastest member of the shark family, capable of speeds approaching 60 miles per hour. The fish are also known for their incredible leaping ability. "It's very common for the makos to clear the water by 20 feet," Conway continued, "and almost every one that we hook jumps. The fish are not at all shy about taking a fly right next to the boat. I try to avoid such scenarios, as I don't want a mako jumping in the boat!"

Suffice it to say, fly fishing for makos is not a dainty game. It begins with chumming. Conway prefers a stew of several salmon carcasses seasoned with menhaden oil—not too messy—hung over the side of the boat in a 5-gallon bucket (like those institutional mayonnaise containers) punched with half-inch holes. Once the boat's in position over a current line, the engine is shut off so as not to put off any finicky fish. Sometimes it takes a while for sharks to appear; sometimes their arrival is almost instantaneous. When the sharks show up in casting range, your fellow angler (or guide) casts a large hookless plug in the vicinity of the shark and retrieves it. This further agitates the already excited shark. As the shark approaches the bait, you prepare to cast—the presentation of the fly should be timed to coincide with the moment the bait is pulled away by your angling partner— the old bait and switch. The flies are big and unwieldy—as large as size 6/0—and need to be landed as close to the shark's eye as possible (they have poor eyesight). But casts seldom need be longer than 30 feet. It's not necessary to strip the fly quickly; a slow ____ven dead drift entices strikes. "When you're fishing for makos, the sharks are ____, not the other way around," Conway said. "They look at you with that big ____nce the fish is hooked, it really takes off. If you haven't hooked a really big fish ____re likely to be overwhelmed. They'll rip 300 yards off the reel, jump two or ____their body length into the air, and often take close to half an hour to land."

____chumming fish in and hooking them with the bait and switch is the most ____ay to fly fish for makos, for a brief window in midsummer, another method ____elf—sight-fishing. "During full moon nights in late July and August, our waters can be as slick as glass," Conway described. "The sharks feed through the night, and then fin around on the surface in the gray light hours. We get up in the middle of the night, so we're out on the water where we've spotted them in the past just before daylight. When we spot a dorsal fin, we'll approach to within 50 or 60 feet with a trolling motor, and then cast a smaller fly—a size 2 to 4/0 toad pattern, in orange and red. You can't tell the size of the shark by the fin, but soon the fish is pursuing the fly as you strip it in, just

OPPOSITE:
Once hooked,
mako sharks can
clear the water by
20 feet or more.

12

DESTINATION

like a tarpon. Suddenly you see the fish—and it could be as big as 300 pounds. Sight-fishing to makos is the ultimate thrill."

Whether sight-fishing or bait and switching, most mako anglers come away from the experience exhilarated . . . but not all. "I had an angler out with me on one occasion who was a trout fisherman," Conway recalled. "We got the chum slick going, and all of a sudden, I saw a huge fin pop out of the water. I said, 'Get ready,' and he replied, 'Okay.' I saw the fish again by the motor—it was more than 300 pounds. I told my guy to cast, but he didn't. Then the fish cruised up our port side, 10 feet away, with one eye staring us down. I don't know if the angler saw the fish before, but he did now. He dropped his rod and said, 'I want to go in right now. This is the spookiest thing I've ever seen.'"

CONWAY BOWMAN is the owner-operator of Bowman Bluewater and a native San Diegan. He began fly fishing in Idaho at eight. Since then, he's mastered the river, lake, and sea. His extensive saltwater experience includes Baja California plus inshore and blue water up and down the West Coast. He has hosted ESPN's *In Search of Flywater* and is the current IGFA world record holder for redfish on 10-pound test with a 41.65 pound red!

If You Go

► **Prime Time:** Makos are present in the greatest concentrations between May and August.

► **Getting There:** San Diego is served by most major carriers. The waters you fish will be in view as you land.

► **Accommodations:** There are many hotels near Mission Bay, where charters depart. A few that Conway recommends include The Dana on Mission Bay (800-445-3339; www.thedana.com), Paradise Point Resort (858-274-4630; www.paradisepoint.com), and the Solana Beach Holiday Inn Express (858-481-9177; www.hiexpress.com).

► **Guides:** Bowman Bluewater Guides and Outfitters (619-822-6256; www.bowman bluewater.com) pioneered this fishery.

► **Equipment:** Your skipper will provide rods and appropriate flies, which are likely to dwarf your entire trout box.

RIO CISNES

RECOMMENDED BY **Tim Purvis**

Fly fishers of the world owe a debt of gratitude to a gentleman named Pedro Golusda. As Adrian Dufflocq, one of the fathers of Chilean fly fishing remembers, Golusda, a German hatchery expert, was retained in 1905 by the government of Chile to bring trout to the Southern Hemisphere. Boarding a steamer with one million fertilized trout and salmon eggs, Golusda made his way south. The boat was scheduled to land at the central Chilean port of Valparaiso (after navigating the Strait of Magellan), but on crossing the equator, Golusda noticed that a significant portion of his charges was nearing maturity. He left the ship with these eggs cum fingerlings and headed overland toward Rio Blanco in Chile, where a new hatchery awaited him. The first fingerlings began hatching a day after his arrival. The fish were soon after introduced to river systems in central and southern Chile, and a world-class fishery was born. It would be a half century before word of the trout-fishing opportunities of Patagonia would reach North America and Europe, largely through the dispatches of Roderick Haig-Brown and Ernest Schwiebert. Today, a sojourn to one of the sprawling estancias of southern Chile or Argentina is a rite of passage for fly anglers, a chance to experience both exquisite fishing and a slice of gaucho life.

As a booking agent who specializes in Patagonia, Tim Purvis has traveled extensively in the region. He explains why Rio Cisnes, in the Aisén Region of Chile (north of the provincial capital of Coyhaique and bordering Argentina), has a special distinction. "On my first visit to Rio Cisnes and Estancia de los Rios," Tim began, "Marcelo and Cristian Dufflocq (sons of Adrian) met me at a wide spot on the main road, and we proceeded to drive up to the ranch. It was a couple of hours' drive up a gravel road—it accentuated the vastness of the land. Being on the east side of the Andes, the land—pampas intersected with winding streams—is drier than you might expect for Chile. With more than 360,000

acres and 60 miles of river and streams divided among ten or twelve guests, you can spread out and get lost in the place. You may see sheep, but you won't see another angler beyond your fishing partner. When we reached the lodge, lunch and Pisco Sours (the unofficial cocktail of Chile, featuring a liquor distilled from grapes) were waiting. Soon after, I was on the river."

The clear air, expansive valleys, and unbelievably blue skies of Chilean Patagonia—all framed by the snowcapped Andes to the west—provide a backdrop that's reminiscent of western Wyoming and Montana . . . albeit, the American Rockies circa 1890 (that is, two years before Jackson Hole was first settled). And the 40 miles of the upper Rio Cisnes (River of the Swans) that flow through the estancia, along with the many spring creeks that dot the property, provide some of the most consistent dry-fly fishing you'll find anywhere. "Through much of the property, the Cisnes meanders slowly through meadows, and it's seldom more than two or three casts across," Tim continued. "Further west, it gains gradient as it enters a canyon en route to the Fjords, where it enters the salt at Puerto Cisnes. Above the canyon it's a shallow, easy-to-wade stream. You seldom need to go in past your knees. It's very graceful, refined fishing. The fish rise quite freely, and when a hatch comes off, trout are on top everywhere. My eyes aren't all they could be, and I don't do little flies easily. But the Cisnes was an absolute delight to fish. I was raised to think that brown trout don't jump, but these fish do. If you fish hard, it's conceivable to have one hundred-fish days, all on dry flies, with a good fish in the high teens. If you're a more advanced angler and want a shot at browns pushing 10 pounds, the guides will be happy to put you on to some beasts . . . but they're extraordinarily wary, and not easy to catch."

One of the attractions of Estancia de los Rios is the variety of angling experiences. Beyond the opportunity to wade the Cisnes, there are the estancia's many spring creeks. "One of the little creeks is called Magdalena," Tim recalled. "It's a one-and-a-half-hour drive away from the main lodge, in a separate valley. To get there, you pass the home of one of the estancia's district managers. In this sparsely inhabited country, it's customary to stop and say hello and share a gourd of maté (a tealike beverage brewed with yerba maté leaves). Eventually you reach Magdalena Creek, which isn't more than 3 feet across in some places, but filled with chunky browns. I fished it with a little 6-foot 3-weight bamboo rod—probably one of the few rivers in the world where you could use such a rod—with little bushy dry flies. Sometimes you cast well back from the stream so you

OPPOSITE:
At Estancia de los Rios, clients have access to 40 miles of the Rio Cisnes. Many sections are quite intimate.

don't spook the fish. There's a little cabin near the creek with a green tin roof where you overnight, and there's a cache of Chilean wine and food waiting when you come off the water. You're roughing it, Patagonia style." In addition to fishing wee spring creeks, you'll have the option to sight-fish to husky browns on one of the lakes scattered around the estancia, or do battle with chinook salmon on Rio Caceres, the main tributary to the Cisnes. (The presence of salmon is an unintended consequence of aquaculture; escapees from salmon farms have colonized at least ten Andean watersheds, according to a report published in the journal *Biological Invasions*.)

As great as the fishing is, it's the ambience of this region of Patagonia that brings people back. One highlight during a stay at Estancia de los Rios is the asado (Argentine-style barbecue). "There's a fire pit in back of the lodge, and a lamb is fixed upon an iron cross," Tim described. "The cross is rotated periodically so the meat is evenly cooked. Some tables are set up, and a few good bottles of red wine—Cabernet Sauvignon, Carmenere, Cabernet Franc—and local empanadas and chorizo are served."

TIM PURVIS grew up fishing in the north of England. Since 1995, Tim has worked arranging custom fly-fishing trips, sending anglers from Bristol Bay, Alaska, to Kamchatka to Iceland to Tierra del Fuego's Rio Grande. In 2009, Tim launched his own booking agency, Andean Anglers (www.andeananglers.com). His firsthand experience with the finest lodges in Chile and Argentina helps him match clients to a memorable angling experience.

If You Go

▶ **Prime Time:** The fishing season in Chile runs from mid-November through April; peak season is generally January to March.

▶ **Getting There:** Guests generally fly to Santiago and then on to Puerto Montt, which is served by LAN Airlines (866-435-9526; www.lan.com).

▶ **Accommodations/Outfitter:** A visit to Rio Cisnes and Estancia de los Rios can be arranged through Andes Journeys (866-999-3218; www.fly-fish-chile.com) or a reputable booking agent, like Andean Anglers (503-703-7323; www.andeananglers.com).

▶ **Equipment:** Ideally, you'll have three rods—a 3-weight, a 5-weight, and a 6-weight, all outfitted with floating lines.

SOUTH PLATTE RIVER

RECOMMENDED BY **Will Rice**

Fly fish for carp? For many anglers, the first response to this question would be "Why?" For coldwater anglers, carp have long been the fodder of bad jokes, a species more likely to be pursued with bow and arrow than beadhead. Recently, however, the fly-fishing frame of mind regarding *Cyprinus carpio* is changing. Will Rice had his day of reckoning, his moment of "carptharsis," a number of years ago.

"During the spring runoff, trout fishing in the Colorado Rockies is pretty much not happening," Will began. "One spring, a friend and I were eager to fish and explore new water, so we headed east from Denver to a reservoir for wiper (a hybrid between striped bass and white bass). We rented a boat and began zipping around. At the edges of the reservoir, high water had pushed over the banks into these large grass flats. We took a closer look and saw big fish—10 to 12 pounds—finning, mudding, even tailing. They were carp, and we spent hours trying to get them to eat a fly. We didn't catch any, but it was eye-opening to see fish behaving like this—the way bonefish and permit behave.

"A few weeks later, my girlfriend (now wife) and I were walking along a trail along the South Platte River in downtown Denver. I looked into the river and saw these big fish poking around in skinny water. I began going down to the river after work with my fly rod; some days I'd even take the rod, along with some wading shoes and a box of flies, into the office and hit the South Platte on the way home. It took me twenty trips before I finally got a fish to eat. I'd begun to think that carp wouldn't eat flies, but then it happened, an 8-pound fish ate an egg-sucking leech just 7 or 8 feet off my rod tip. I remember standing on the edge of river in the middle of Denver with my hands in the air."

American fly anglers are beginning to recognize what British fishermen have long understood: that carp are finicky and easily put off by a poor cast, but will respond to a

DESTINATION 14

well-presented fly and are the equal of large steelhead and sometimes even bonefish when it comes to tearing line off your reel. It's the latter comparison that has gained carp the moniker "golden ghost." Ask any number of guides on the finest trout streams in the American West what they do on their days off, and very often they'll say they chase carp. "There's a pretty common story line for guys who get whacked out on carp," Will continued. "They start out fly fishing for trout, and then take a saltwater trip where they catch bonefish and tarpon. In the course of the saltwater fishing, something clicks about getting bigger fish on the fly. When they get back home and fish for trout again, that big fish thrill is a little lacking. Then they discover carp. There are a lot of similarities between carp fishing and exotic saltwater fly fishing, but carp venues are a lot closer to home."

The South Platte River has a fine trout-fishing pedigree in its reaches upstream of Chatfield Reservoir (near the suburb of Littleton), but once it reaches Denver, there are few salmonids in sight. Instead, the South Platte is home to what the British gently call "coarse" fish, and what many American sportfishers indelicately refer to as "trash" fish— for its nearly 400 miles from Denver, across eastern Colorado, and into Nebraska to its confluence with the North Platte. Between its banks in greater Denver, no one would mistake the South Platte for an idyllic trout stream. It's easy to dismiss the river as "Denver's drainage ditch"; indeed, several sections of the city adjoining the river have been targeted as brownfield redevelopment areas. Yet a variety of groups, ranging from Trout Unlimited to the U.S. Army Corps of Engineers, have worked diligently to revitalize the South Platte as a recreational area. Bike and pedestrian paths follow much of the river through its urban corridor. And when the flows are right, the South Platte runs clear enough for anglers to sight-fish to urban leviathans in the shadow of Invesco Stadium (home of the NFL's Broncos).

"Fishing the South Platte is unquestionably an urban experience," Will added. "One of my favorite pools has a large homeless encampment nearby, and I've had one or two occasions when people have tried to walk off with my bike. You see all sorts of folks walking the pedestrian trail; many will call out, 'What are you doin' with a fly rod?' When they look a little harder and see the carp finning in the current, their response is 'Whoa!'"

Carp are catholic feeders—they'll feast on aquatic insects in all life stages, crayfish, baitfish, and even plant matter, such as blackberries. One shouldn't mistake the carp's broad appetite as license for sloppy presentations, though. Carp possess highly developed senses of sight, hearing, touch, and smell. This makes them extremely spooky. A spooked fish emits a pheromone that warns other nearby fish of potential danger. If you misfire and put one fish off, odds are good that any other fish in the immediate region will go off the bite as well. "On the South Platte, I believe the fish are mostly eating crawfish, so I rely on crawfish or crab imitations—the latter the same flies I use for permit," Will said. "More important than the fly, though, is finding a fish that's actually feeding, as opposed to sunning itself or just cruising.

"In the end, it's all about watching the take. Seeing a carp chase a fly across a river and punch it is as cool as watching a bonefish pick up a Crazy Charlie. When you set the hook, they don't even know what's going on; they just continue on their way. When they do realize that something's wrong, the water just explodes, and they're gone. The big ones roll off slowly like an eighteen-wheeler in low gear. The smaller fish can melt line off the reel in bursts. One in four times I go out, I can get a fish to eat. It's always a little different. And it's never really easy."

WILL RICE is a contributing editor for *Drake Magazine* and a contributor to the *Denver Post, Flyfish Journal, Angling Trade,* and *Colorado Fish Explorer.* He grew up fishing for bass in upstate New York, but has been based in Colorado since 1995. In addition to angling across the western United States, Will's travels and species exploration have taken him fishing in Chile, Argentina, Belize, the Bahamas, Tortola, and Mexico.

If You Go

▶ **Prime Time:** The Denver chapter of Trout Unlimited hosts the annual Carp Slam (www.carpslam.org) each August to raise funds for South Platte restoration projects.

▶ **Getting There:** Denver is served by most major carriers.

▶ **Accommodations:** The Denver Convention and Visitors Bureau (800-233-6837; www.denver.org) lists a broad range of lodging options in the Mile High City.

▶ **Guides:** Colorado Trouthunters (303-325-5515; www.coloradotrouthunters.com) can set you up with everything you need.

▶ **Equipment:** An 8-weight rod outfitted with a floating line and 200 yards of backing will handle South Platte carp. Will likes to use crab and crayfish patterns.

RIO BLANCO

RECOMMENDED BY **Jim Hill**

Rio Blanco tumbles out of a range of 12,000-foot-tall mountains in the San Juan National Forest, 20 miles southeast of Pagosa Springs, Colorado, into a beautiful valley that's reminiscent of a miniature Yosemite. In its upper reaches, the Blanco runs in a white-water cascade and is home to native cutthroat trout. In the valley, the water slows and deepens, providing excellent habitat for introduced rainbows that frequently exceed 20 inches.

But it wasn't always that way.

"I had been fishing and guiding with Damon Scott for ten years," Jim Hill recalled. "When Damon became manager of El Rancho Pinoso [which encompasses much of the valley and the prime stretches of Rio Blanco], he asked me to go with him to take a look. When we saw what had been done, we were both in awe. Much of the river had not historically been conducive to fishing, thanks to flooding off the mountains. The channel was extremely spread out—there was simply not enough holding water. Now there was a great variety of water that would hold trout—pools, runs, and riffles. The revitalized river—combined with the scenery—has given me a spectacular office to work from."

For some, the notion of a river that's felt the shaping hand of man is mildly distasteful, like an overly manicured garden or a dunes-laden golf course fabricated from thousands of tons of imported dirt. For Dave Rosgen of Wildland Hydrology, it's potential realized. "When I first visited Rancho Pinoso, it seemed like the valley was one big gravel bar," Rosgen said. "The Blanco was anywhere from 350 to 500 feet wide, when it should be 50 or 60 feet wide. As it was, you had a system that had no hope to be anything but a very poor fishery; with a little help, you could have a stream that followed a natural system that gives trout an opportunity to thrive, and people a chance to feel good." To engineer

OPPOSITE: Set in an incredibly beautiful southwestern Colorado valley, Rio Blanco may be the most beautiful man-made trout stream you'll ever fish.

73

the changes necessary to make the Rio Blanco a viable fishery, Rosgen researched other healthy rivers in the region to find a system that had a similar flow regime, and hence was naturally stable. After finding such a model river, he began to map out a blueprint for the Blanco—though before the riverbed and banks could be refashioned, Rosgen needed a way to filter out the massive amounts of sediment carried downstream from the mountains. "We constructed a sediment tube to divert cobble, gravel, and sand away from the river channel," Rosgen explained. "The sediment is routed to a holding pond that can be emptied out each year, with the gravel used to supplement roads and trails." The result is a trout stream that's as fecund as it is beautiful.

Guests at El Rancho Pinoso have the exclusive run of 3 miles of the Rio Blanco, which can be accessed from the ranch's two handsome log cabins in a five-minute stroll. (The ranch and its waters are generally available to one group at a time to ensure an intimate experience.) "In the wilderness, you can find good spots to fish, but it takes some time to hike or float in," Jim continued. "At Rancho Pinoso, you can show people who have a limited amount of time some great fishing in a spectacular setting. It's a wonderful spot for beginners, as we can work with them on the lawn to get the rudiments of the cast down, and then move them into the river and catch fish—often on dry flies. The rainbows are often very susceptible to an Adams or Pale Morning Dun. We had two couples visiting from California last year. The wives had never fished. The plan was that the wives would get a casting lesson and fish long enough to land one trout. Before noon, the ladies had caught fish. They enjoyed it so much, they insisted on fishing for the remainder of the trip.

"Another thing I love about the river is that the wading is very easy. Thanks to Dave's work, the gravel beds are such that people without very good balance can still negotiate the river. We have a lot of older father and son visitors, and it's a perfect match; the sons in their forties or fifties can do some fishing with their dads, who are in their seventies or eighties, and can also fish hard on their own."

It may be difficult to tear yourself away from Rancho Pinoso, but steel your nerves and do so—because an equally beautiful valley awaits roughly an hour to the northwest, in the San Juan Mountains. Here, on another secluded ranch, 7 miles of the Weminuche River await your exploration. The Weminuche twists and turns through a broad meadow, and hosts brown as well as rainbow trout, with most fish between 16 and 21 inches—and some browns topping 25 inches. The lower stretches on the property (owned by the Lindner family, which also owns Rancho Pinoso) have benefitted from Dave Rosgen's restoration work; the upper stretches have not been sculpted. The fishing on both sections is superb. "I first came to the Weminuche fifty-five years ago," Jim recalled. "It was a graduation present from my dad. Having the chance to guide here all these years later is very special. What's been done in terms of restoration on the lower section to help it hold more and larger fish makes it far more appealing a fishery than I remember. A nice thing about streams that have been structured is that they're easier for novices to understand. On the Weminuche, we keep the beginners on the lower section for that reason.

"But if the guest can make long, accurate casts and keep a big fish out of the roots, we love to take them upstream, where things are a little tighter. The hopper fishing up there in the late summer and fall can be explosive—just drop it in the pocket and hold on!"

JIM HILL began fishing when he was a child in New Mexico in the 1940s, and took up fly fishing while attending University of Colorado. Since that time he's fly fished extensively throughout the west, as well as in the Bahamas, Belize, New Zealand, south Texas, and Florida. One of his favorite destinations is northern British Columbia, where he loves to chase steelhead. Jim, now retired from the insurance business, has been guiding in the Four Corners region of southwestern Colorado since 2001.

If You Go

▶ **Prime Time:** Rio Blanco and the Weminuche are open for fishing for guests of El Rancho Pinoso from mid-June through September.

▶ **Getting There:** The closest commercial airport is in Durango, which is served by several carriers, including Frontier Airlines (800-432-1359; www.frontierairlines.com). Albuquerque (four hours' drive) and Denver (six hours' drive) are two other options.

▶ **Accommodations/Guides:** Guests at El Rancho Pinoso (888-801-1097; www.elrancho pinoso.com) stay in one of the property's two restored log cabins. Guides are included. Bookings are through Fly Water Travel (800-552-2729; www.flywatertravel.com).

▶ **Equipment:** A 5-weight rod outfitted with a floating line will work for all the rivers around El Rancho Pinoso. Fly Water Travel can provide a list of proven patterns.

DERBYSHIRE WYE

RECOMMENDED BY **Dr. John Smith**

Much of the lore of early English fly fishing—which is to say, *early fly fishing*—revolves around the chalk streams of Hampshire, most notably the Test and the Ichen. It was here, after all, that Izaak Walton's Piscator cavorted among the region's "swift, shallow, clear, pleasant brooks, and store of Trouts," as immortalized in the *Compleat Angler*.

Or was it?

"It can be argued that Derbyshire, not Hampshire, is the cradle of trout fishing," declared John Smith. "Izaak Walton was born in the region, and Charles Cotton—who contributed a section on fly fishing to the 1676 edition of the *Compleat Angler*—called the Dove his home river. Huge volumes have been written about Frederick Halford and the evolution of the dry fly from Halford's fishing in Hampshire. The fact is, there were two other gentlemen fishing dry flies in the 1850s—some thirty years before the publication of *Floating Flies and How to Dress Them* [published in 1886]. These fellows—David Foster and James Ogden—fished many of the rivers of Derbyshire with their creations—among them, the Wye. At this time, anglers would fish 18- or 20-foot rods with horse hair affixed to the top of the rod, and live mayflies for bait. Ogden is said to have appeared on the banks of the Wye at Haddon Estate [toward the bottom of the river] with an artificial fly affixed to his rod—a pattern quite similar to what we know today. I feel quite privileged to tread in the footsteps of Walton, Cotton, Ogden, and Foster."

The Derbyshire Wye is a short stream, rising above the town of Buxton and burbling 15 miles before joining the Derwent, at the town of Rowsley. "The Wye rests at the bottom end of the Pennines in England's Peak District," John continued. "Water collects among the limestone peaks and cliffs, accumulates in aquifers and underground caverns and emerges to the surface through a series of five springs. Its consistent cold temperature and high alkaline content [courtesy of the limestone] are conducive to weed growth—water crowfoot and the like—which in turn creates classic habitat for mayflies. In this sense, the Wye is analogous to the chalk streams in the south. In its upper sections, it flows through limestone gorges and has more of a wild, up-country feeling. In the lower stretches, the river has a more pastoral setting—not exactly the cultivated water meadows you find on the chalk streams, but still quite bucolic, with sheep dotting the green fields." Depending on which beat you fish, you may come upon stock scenes of English country beauty— stone bridges, riverside pubs, and perhaps the Monsal Dale viaduct.

As you'd expect on an English stream, brown trout are a significant quarry on the Derbyshire Wye. But unlike most UK rivers, the Wye supports a vibrant population of wild rainbows. "The story goes," John explained, "that in the late 1890s, the then owner of the Haddon Estate imported some rainbow fry from the United States and stocked them into a nearby Ashford lake. Some of the grown fry escaped into the Wye as a result of floods and established a breeding population in the river. Their iridescent purple splotches and russet-tipped dorsal fins make them a uniquely handsome fish—and the opportunity to fish for wild rainbows in England is special."

The Wye's rainbows (and browns and grayling, for that matter) need bugs to eat, and one of its riverkeepers has embarked on a unique experiment—stocking mayflies to replenish extant varieties. "In the late 1960s, there was a pollution incident on the river," John said. "As a result, many of our trout were killed. And the mayflies [*Ephemera danica*] that regularly emerged on the upper portions of the river were all but destroyed. The recently retired riverkeeper for the section of the Wye I fish [Cressbrook & Litton]—David Percival—decided that these insects could be repopulated. After capturing mature nymphs and spinners from downstream, he planted the nymphs in the river and managed to capture spinner eggs on glass tiles that were suspended in the river. He also propagated nymphs in glass jars and released them into the river. Thus far, the project seems to have been a great success."

When asked how a typical summer's day on the Wye unfolds, John was happy to elaborate. "We generally don't get to the river until about ten, as there's not much insect activity before then. You'll assemble at one of the huts to meet other anglers. Fishing during our mayfly hatch—what American anglers might call green drakes—will begin around lunchtime, with the trout focusing on emerging and hatching duns until mid-afternoon. There's a little break for anglers and fish until the spinners begin mating. Once they mate, die, and fall on the water, fishing begins again in earnest and can last into the evening. Once the fishing is done, we like to adjourn to one of the local pubs. My fellow anglers favor The Red Lion, The Waterloo, The Bull's Head, and The Horse & Jockey."

A most fitting way to conclude a fine day on a great English spring creek!

DR. JOHN FREDERICK HERBERT SMITH is a member of good standing of The Flyfishers' Club, London, and of the Cressbrook & Litton Flyfishers. His angling adventures have taken him from Iceland to Belize to New Zealand, though he's always happy to return to his beloved Wye. "I was born and grew up in Salisbury, Wiltshire, on a river called the Nadder, which is a tributary of the Avon." The river is famous for its association with Frank Sawyer, inventor of the Sawyer's nymph, and Olive Kite, who did much to promote techniques for upstream nymphing. One of his middle names—Herbert—comes from George Herbert, a priest and poet from the 1600s. Herbert occasionally crossed paths with Izaak Walton; Walton, in fact, wrote a biography of Herbert. Smith was baptized in the church where Herbert was once the rector and ended up walking the same rivers in Derbyshire as his biographer. When he's not fishing, John is a gynecological surgical pathologist and cytopathologist at the Royal Hallamshire Hospital, Sheffield.

If You Go

▶ **Prime Time:** The season runs from early March through early October. Early June is usually the peak of the dry-fly season.

▶ **Getting There:** The Derbyshire Wye is most easily reached from Manchester, England, which has service from most major international carriers.

▶ **Accommodations:** The Peak District and Derbyshire website (www.visitpeakdistrict .com) highlights area accommodations. Riverside rooms are available at The Peacock at Rowsley (+44 1629 733 518; www.thepeacockatrowsley.com).

▶ **Guides/Outfitters:** Daily beats are available from the Cressbrook & Litton Flyfishers' Club (+44 1298 871 676; www.cressbrookandlittonflyfishers.co.uk). The Peacock at Rowsley (see above) also has beats available for visitors.

▶ **Equipment:** A lighter rod (in the 3- to 5-weight range) with floating line is the right stick for the Wye. The riverkeepers on each stretch can help you with fly selections.

HOMOSASSA SPRINGS

RECOMMENDED BY **Mac McKeever**

"When I picked up fly fishing as a kid, I'd look at the magazines of the day—*Sports Afield*, *Outdoor Life*, etc.," Mac McKeever began. "I was drawn to articles on larger fish—pike, largemouth bass, and, eventually, tarpon. I became obsessed with tarpon, reading everything I could about the silver giants. When I was twelve, my family took a trip to Marathon, down in the Keys, and I was lucky enough to jump some fish with an 11-weight fly rod I'd made. The fish were 5 or 6 feet long; I was forever changed!

"When I became an adult, I visited Florida as much as I could to chase tarpon and other game fish, fly fishing from the Keys to Sanibel Island. Six or seven years ago, I visited Homosassa for the first time. A friend took me out to a well-known spot called Oklahoma Flat, off Pine Island—and the tarpon fleet unfolded before us. You can see the fleet from several miles off—specks on the horizon—from twenty to forty tarpon skiffs, pirouetting as they're being poled around. The boats are decked out with poling towers, the anglers are clad in high-tech clothes. It's strangely quiet. People will wave, but they don't say anything. Tarpon are rolling here and there. Then, a fish will be jumped in the distance. You'll see the glint of the animal's scales, hear the sound of the fish crashing back into the water. You know that the guys around you are some of the top anglers in the world, working with some of the top guides. And you realize that this is *the game*."

Anyone who has seriously pursued tarpon dreams of fishing the flats of greater Homosassa in May and June for a chance to hook into a "giant" tarpon (a fish of 120 pounds or more) or a "toad that pushes the mark" (a tarpon approaching the mythic weight of 200 pounds). Homosassa is a sleepy town on the Florida coast north of Tampa—sleepy, that is, until the silver kings begin to arrive. "Homosassa is atypical of Florida, in that it's very quiet and undeveloped," Mac continued. "But for two months of

the year, it's totally dedicated to tarpon. It's pretty much the center of the saltwater fly-fishing universe. It's fun to be there immersed in the tarpon culture."

The famed tarpon grounds of Homosassa extend some 25 miles, from the Crystal River in the north to Chassahowitzka Bay and Pine Island in the south. No one knows exactly why the big fish frequent this region each spring, though it's widely believed that the infusion of freshwater from the cool, clear rivers that feed into the Gulf of Mexico here have a lot to do with it. "The water has this crystalline, emerald quality that results from spring-fed rivers," Mac said. "It's very distinctive, different from the water on any other flats I've visited. One conjecture for the tarpon presence here is that the mix of fresh and salt water has historically created an ideal habitat for crabs, which the fish seem to target; in the past, caught fish would spit up crabs. In recent years, the fish population has ebbed. Some feel it's because the flow from the springs has changed, creating a level of salinity that's detracted from crab habitat. Others think it's angling pressure."

It was on the flats of Homosassa that, for all intents and purposes, the sport of fly fishing for tarpon was born. Fittingly enough, the first angler to land a giant tarpon on a fly here was Lefty Kreh. By the late seventies, word was officially out. "Back in the good old days, it was not unheard of for the best anglers to jump fifty fish in a day," Mac added. "You don't hear reports like this anymore, but the big fish are still around. A guy named Jim Holland Jr. landed a 202.5-pound fish in 2001, just north of town. I've seen fish pushing 200 pounds swim right past my boat. To know that your fly is a few feet away from a fish like that is incredibly exhilarating . . . whether they eat it or not. When they do eat, it's remarkable. The fish's body language tells you it's tracking the fly. As the fish rises toward the bug, its mouth opens, and you swear it could eat a soccer ball. After the eat, there are thirty seconds of pure chaos. Looking that fish in the eye as it leaps to your height (or above!), hearing the gills rattle like banging trash cans—it's life altering."

If having a shot at a toad that pushes the mark is one of fly fishing's seminal moments, it's also one that can be fraught with anxiety, thanks in no small part to the expectations of your guide. "Stern" and "focused" are two words that sportfishers have used to describe their Homosassa guides; others are less printable. "There's no question it's intense out there," Mac continued. "The guides want you to catch a fish more than you do, and the best guides take their job very seriously."

On his first visit to Homosassa, Mac felt well prepared . . . until the first fish appeared. "I was fishing with a good friend who happens to be a famous angler," Mac recalled. "He

OPPOSITE: Giant tarpon (fish that push the 120-pound mark) focus the saltwater-angling world's attention on Homosassa each spring.

led us to a spot where a group of giant, lumbering fish were laid up. I must have blown a half dozen shots. My friend was very patient, but I felt terrible. These fish bring out the worst in people, and my intimidation was made even worse by the presence of a legend in the boat. The next day, we returned to the same spot, and two giants were laid up again, one 130 pounds, the other 150. This time I made a perfect cast, and both started following the fly. The smaller fish then rushed up and ate the fly 15 feet from the boat. We came tight and my friend said, 'Hit him!' I did; the fish was high in the air, 30 feet away. It landed with a 'KABOOM,' and soon had stripped off 200 yards of line. My friend said, 'You're doing a great job, you're going to get him.'

"He was right. I did."

MAC MCKEEVER is a senior public relations specialist with L.L. Bean, a $1.5 billion outdoor specialty retailer. He represents the entire fishing, hunting, and outdoor gear and apparel divisions across the catalog, Internet, and retail channels. Prior to that, Mac headed up all of the advertising, marketing, and public relations activities for the L.L. Bean Outdoor Discovery Schools, a 23,000-plus-participant-per-year outfitter. He has extensive experience with television production including local, regional, and national hunting and fishing shows (production and guest appearances), advertisements, and videos. When he's not chasing tarpon, Mac loves to stalk striped bass near Portland, Maine.

If You Go

▶ **Prime Time:** Count on the big toads around Homosassa in May and June.

▶ **Getting There:** Homosassa is roughly 60 miles from Tampa, which is served by most major domestic carriers.

▶ **Accommodations:** The Citrus County Visitors & Convention Bureau (800-587-6667; www.visitcitrus.com) lists accommodations around Homosassa.

▶ **Guides:** Guides that Mac has fished with include Captain Jim Long (352-795-3156), Captain Dan Malzone (813-832-4052), and Captain Mike Locklear (352-422-1927).

▶ **Equipment:** A 12-weight rod with the best saltwater reel you can afford outfitted with floating and intermediate lines, 300 yards of backing, and 80-pound shock tippet (with 16- to 20-pound bite tippet). Your guide will have the right flies for your tarpon assault.

PUERTO SAN JOSÉ

RECOMMENDED BY **Chuck Furimsky**

Chuck Furimsky had always wanted to catch a sailfish on a fly. Eventually his quest took him to Guatemala. "Jake Jordan [a celebrated Florida Keys tarpon guide and fly-fishing presenter] had been telling me about the fishery for years," Chuck began. "The way he described the fishery, it sounded just crazy. One year he had had fifty clients down to Guatemala—some only for a day or two—and every single angler had hooked and landed a billfish. Some of these people were very inexperienced anglers. I figured that I'd been fly fishing most of my life, and that I was better than average—so I should be able to catch one too. The notion of catching a fish as long as me was an exciting proposition."

Thanks to the on-again, off-again revolution/civil war that tore at the country for nearly fifty years, Guatemala has not attracted as much tourist interest as neighboring Belize and Mexico's Yucatán Peninsula. Yet the small nation has much to offer, including nineteen different ecosystems (from mangrove swamps to lowland jungles to high woodlands), rich Mayan ruin sites, active volcanoes, tremendous bird life, and a friendly citizenry that warmly embraces visitors. (A peace accord was struck between warring factions in 1998, making travel more feasible for those uninterested in ducking the occasional insurgent bullet.) Billfishers have long known of Guatemala's sailfish bounty and have been making the trek to the nation's Pacific coast since before reconciliation was reached. It's all in the numbers. It's not uncommon for fly anglers to have more than a dozen shots at sailfish in a given day, with an average of 5 to 8 fish landed; on one memorable outing, a group of fly fishers on one boat landed 57 . . . in one day! (The record using conventional tackle is 124 fish.) Fish average between 60 and 90 pounds, though individuals approaching 200 pounds are caught each year. As the National Oceanic and Atmospheric Administration has documented, even the worst year of sailfish catches in Guatemala were far better than

the best years at other North and Central American fisheries. Currents and prevailing winds conspire to attract a potpourri of baitfish to the Guatemalan coast, which in turn draw in pelagic species in the upper sections of the water column. Ideal conditions are abetted by a farsighted (and strictly enforced) catch-and-release policy for sportfishers and a prohibition on commercial billfishing.

Chuck's pilgrimage for his first sailfish began on a calm, clear December day. "We only had to run out about a half hour to be in very deep water," Chuck continued. "One of the appeals of going to Guatemala is that the waters are almost always very calm, and the runs are short—both positives, as I don't enjoy going way offshore and fishing in rough water. As we were heading out, Jake gave us a briefing on what to expect. He said, 'I'll hook the first fish to show you how it's done.'" The drill goes something like this: The captain and his mates—all unbelievably knowledgeable—have three or four lines with teaser plugs out. When a fish shows, the captain calls down to let the mates know which line the fish is following. Everyone jumps into motion. One mate quickly reels in the other teaser baits and the other mate slowly reels in the bait the fish is on. The captain then tells you to cast out your line—about 25 feet. When the fish gets close, the captain puts the boat into neutral and the mate brings the plug close to the fly. The angler then water loads the line and makes the cast. The mate pulls the plug away as the fly hits the water, and the fish hears the fly, and soon sees it—a huge Cam Ziegler creation in hot pink. When the fish takes the fly, you point the rod right at the fish and set the hook by pulling back on the rod—not up, but straight back. When the sailfish feels the hook, it explodes out of the water and is off to the races. It's not uncommon for the fish to leap six or seven times, and to take out 200 or 300 yards of backing.

"That day, it wasn't even twenty minutes before the first sailfish was in the wash of the boat," Chuck said. "The mates drew it close, and Jake made the cast. Everything was textbook. Working closely with the captain [who positioned the boat to facilitate a fast landing], Jake had the fish to hand in just eight minutes. My turn came, and I also hooked up. It's really something when that fish clears the water 20 feet away from the boat. I didn't know whether to laugh or scream—it's an unbelievable experience. You need to keep pointing the rod at the fish. The drag is set perfectly, so you can maintain some pressure on the fish without snapping your leader. One thing you need to look out for in the fight—when the fish jumps, it sends a wave through the line, and it could make a wind knot over the rod tip and bust it."

OPPOSITE:
Finding a sailfish on the fly off Guatemala is virtually a guarantee; on his first outing, Chuck Furimsky's boat landed twenty-two!

Anglers on a boat—usually two or three—take turns on point. If you make a cast and the fish refuses or you miss the set, you sit down and the next guy comes up. On Chuck's first day, the group shifted quickly, as twenty-two fish were landed. On several occasions, anglers had two fish on simultaneously. "Sometimes when you're fighting a fish, a second or third fish shows up," Chuck explained. "The mates keep a spinning rod rigged with a ballyhoo [local baitfish] on hand. They can toss the ballyhoo out if a fish loses interest in the teaser plug, or if other fish appear while a fish is being played. Jake had a fish on at one point, and I managed to hook one as well. My fish jumped, and the line wrapped around my rod tip. My rod came undone, but the fish was still on. It jumped right over the boat's stern, spraying us. I knocked one of the mate's hats into the water as I tried to keep up. 'Fight the fish with the butt of your rod!' the captain yelled. The fish jumped again, and the top half of the rod came back up the fly line. The mate grabbed it and got the rod back together . . . and both Jake and I got our fish in.

"Near the end of this unbelievable day, my son Ben landed his ninth sailfish of the day. It was flat calm, and Jake asked Ben if he wanted to jump in and pose with his fish. He said, 'Sure!' Ben shed his shirt and sunglasses and grabbed one of the gloves that the mates use to land the fish, and jumped in. He posed with the fish just the way you see guys posing with tarpon in the water—except the water here was hundreds of feet deep. He held the bill with the gloved hand and had his other arm around the body. After a moment the fish started to sound. Ben held on for a moment, then watched the fish swim away from underneath the water."

CHUCK FURIMSKY is the director and chief executive officer of the Fly Fishing Show, which he founded with Barry Serviente, nearly twenty years ago. Today, it's the largest fly-fishing-specific exposition in the United States, currently operating eight shows around the country. Chuck began fishing as a young boy in McKeesport, Pennsylvania, and developed his fly-fishing skills under the late, great George Harvey while attending Penn State. Chuck is an avid fly tier; he's the sole director of the International Fly Tyers Symposium and designs flies for Rainy's Flies. He's developed a tying material made from leather called Bugskin. Chuck never misses the opening day of trout season in Pennsylvania and enjoys a calm day at sea off the coast of New Jersey on his boat *Ole Man Winter*.

If You Go

▶ **Prime Time:** The waters off San José fish well from October through June; fall months tend to yield larger fish, the winter and spring generally yield bigger numbers.

▶ **Getting There:** Most visitors will fly into Guatemala City, which is in the Highlands region and is served by many major carriers, including American Airlines (800-433-7300; www.aa.com), Continental Airlines (800-523-3273; www.continental.com), and Delta Airlines (800-221-1212; www.delta.com). From the airport, it's a ninety-minute drive to Puerto San José.

▶ **Accommodations/Outfitters:** Several properties around Puerto San José cater to anglers, but Casa Vieja (866-846-9121; www.casaviejalodge.com) has built a fine reputation catering to fly anglers. The hotel has a fine restaurant and bar and offers all-inclusive packages (with transfer to and from the airport and well-appointed boats). Jake Jordan (252-444-3308; www.jakejordan.com) conducts Sailfish Fly Fishing Schools from Casa Vieja throughout the winter.

▶ **Equipment:** If you fish out of Casa Vieja, all gear is provided. If you want to bring your own, a 12-weight with floating line is the ticket; flies and leaders will be provided.

18

DESTINATION

OAHU

RECOMMENDED BY **Mike Hennessy**

Picture in your mind's eye a world-class bonefishing flat. Chances are good that it's not framed by brilliant green mountains. Chances are even better that it's not within eye- and earshot of a bustling port, replete with cranes and container ships.

But that's just what you encounter on the Hawaiian island of Oahu. More important, amid these uncharacteristic (and in the case of the port, slightly surreal) surroundings, you'll find what may be your best odds anywhere for hooking up with a double-digit bone.

"When I was a munchkin, my dad had a sailboat on Kane'ohe Bay on the east side of the island," Mike Hennessy began. "We used to take the boat out to a sandbar in the bay and anchor up. We'd sometimes don scuba gear and clean the bottom of the boat, and we'd see schools of huge bonefish. Sometimes we'd put scraps of salami or whatever we had left over from lunch on a hook and catch them. When I was finished with school, I left Hawaii to start an eco lodge in Costa Rica, and there I took up saltwater fly fishing. I was gone for fourteen years, but I said to myself that if I ever got back to Hawaii, I would have to start fly fishing for those big bonefish I used to see around the sailboat. Circumstances brought me back, and I happened to hook up with a fly-fishing guide named Dave Hill, who split his time between Montana and Oahu. Dave really had the bonefishing wired. With Dave's help, I was able to begin targeting the big bones on the fly. On the average day, we'll see two to six fish in the double-digit range, and generally get at least one or two good shots."

While bonefish range throughout the warm waters that surround Hawaii, the challenge for fly casters is to find water shallow enough to pursue them. The steep nature of the island's above-water topography extends into the ocean, and the drop-offs are immense. There are a few exceptions to this rule—Kauai boasts a fishable flat, and Maui has a few. But neither of these islands can compete with Oahu, which boasts a number of pancake flats during cooperative tides. A number are situated in scenic Kaneʻohe Bay, with the Koʻolau Mountains to the west and Marine Corps Base Hawaii to the east. (Anglers fishing the early morning tide may be treated to "Reveille" as they tread the flats.) A few other flats are just off downtown Honolulu—"the industrial war zone," as Mike jokingly referred to this unlikely urban fishery.

The oversize bonefish that haunt the flats of Oahu—fish so big that when tailers flop over, they send a plume of water 3 feet in the air—did not get so big by being gullible. While bonefish everywhere can be skittish, Oahu bones (oʻio in local parlance) are particularly finicky. "For starters, you have to master good stalking techniques," Mike continued. "There's a lot of coral on our flats, and you have to try to avoid it, as the fish can hear the crunch of coral from 50 yards away. They can pick up even subtler sounds. I had one fellow not long ago who was wearing long pants. The legs were trapping air bubbles, and I could see that the bubbles were spooking fish 80 feet away. He unzipped the bottom half and we hung them on some mangroves. Without the long pants, we were able to sneak within 15 feet of the fish."

The feeding habits of big Oahu bones differ somewhat from their Caribbean brethren. "We were fishing the downtown flats one evening, and after a half hour my buddy said, 'I don't think they're eating shrimp tonight.' We turned around and watched a big fish slurping little goatfish off the surface. When we switched over to a Mai Tai Clouser, we began hooking up. A friend who works in the bonefish-tagging program at the University of Hawaii has analyzed stomach contents of some fish. She found that 10 percent of their diet was baitfish—immature goatfish or lizardfish, gobies, etc. The other 90 percent was mantis shrimp, ghost shrimp, crabs, and sea slugs. To fit what you're fishing and the bones' mood on a given day, you have to adapt presentations a great deal. Some days, the hoop for your cast is 2 feet from the fish's head. Other times, it's 30 feet. Likewise, you will need to vary the speed and cadence of your strip. Strip-strip-strip might not do it, but strip-stop-strip might work. Some weeks, presentation is 90 percent of the game and the fly is 10 percent; others, it's 90 percent fly, 10 percent presentation."

When you hook a fish on the flats of Oahu, the game has just begun. Nearly all the flats are bordered by coral and deep water, and when one of the big guys is hooked, that's where it heads. If your leader—even with 20-pound tippet—scrapes against the coral, you're done. "When you fool a fish into taking your fly, you get an advanced degree in bonefishing," Mike said. "When you can stop the fish after a 100-yard run when the fish wants to go 200 yards, you get your PhD." It's not unheard of for anglers to take to the cuts and channels to free fish from the coral so they have a chance to eventually claim their prize.

"I had a couple guys fishing a flat," Mike recalled. "I sent one of the anglers over behind some mangroves while I untangled the other fellow's leader. Suddenly the first guy is screaming. I thought a tiger shark had wandered onto the flats, but he'd hooked into a big fish. The fish is tearing out line, heading toward the reef, and this fellow is running after him, right toward us. The fish leaves the flat, and I tell the guy to throw his reel in free spool to relieve any tension on the line. The three of us got up to the edge of the flat, and it's apparent that the fish has wrapped around something on the drop-off, about 8 or 10 feet down. I offered to dive in and unwrap it, but he said, 'No. It's my fish, I've got to do it myself.' So his buddy held the rod, and he dove in and unwrapped the line from the coral head. The fish was still on—but it immediately ran out to an old machine gun turret post that's off the flat, and ran around that. This time he dove in with rod in hand. I could only see his rod, hat, and sunglasses. He was reeling as he swam. He got the line untangled from the turret, made it back to the flat, and landed the fish. It wasn't the 10-pounder he was hoping for [just 8.5 pounds], but I'm pretty confident that it was the most rewarding fish he's ever caught."

CAPTAIN MIKE HENNESSY caught his first striped marlin with his dad in Cabo San Lucas at the age of ten. Soon after he was charter fishing in Newport Beach, California, on half-day and full-day boats. Fly fishing in the High Sierras was also a passion that started early in his life and continues to this day. By the age of nineteen, he had earned his 100-ton masters license and was competing with seasoned peers and of course the fish scales. Since then he has been following his dream to catch the biggest and best fish and experiences around the world. Always looking for adventure, Mike headed down to the southern zone of Costa Rica in 1995, and for twelve years he led Cabo Matapalo Sportfishing on a 28-foot Carolina Classic. They released hundreds of big blue and black marlin and thousands of sailfish, taking home some of the area's top tournament trophies on conventional tackle as well as on the fly. Fly fishing inshore for snook and offshore for big game on the fly kept the fly-fishing bug going in the tropics. Fishing has taken him to five continents. Now based in Oahu, Mike guides his clients to trophy bonefish and other prize species on the fly. He is an IGFA Certified Captain and has been featured on the Outdoor Channel and in many publications, including *Center Console, Saltwater, and Marlin.*

▶ **Prime Time:** The big bonefish of Oahu are present throughout the year. It can often be windy on the leeward (eastern) side of the island, but with sunshine, fish can still be spotted.

▶ **Getting There:** Oahu (Honolulu) is served by most major carriers.

▶ **Accommodations:** The Oahu Visitors Bureau (www.visit-oahu.com) provides an overview of the many lodging options on this popular vacation getaway. (Staying on the east side of the island will put you closer to most of the fishing.)

▶ **Guides:** Mike's company, Hawaii On the Fly (808-366-7835; www.hawaiionthefly.com), and Coach Duff (808-292-9680) target bonefish around Oahu. There's also freshwater fishing for peacock bass.

▶ **Equipment:** An 8-weight rod with the best reel you can afford with floating line and at least 250 yards of 30-pound backing will work. (Some anglers may prefer a 9-weight for windy days.)

DESTINATION 19

UPPER LAXÁ I ADALDAL

RECOMMENDED BY **Peter McLeod**

Readers of *Fifty Places to Fly Fish Before You Die* may recognize the name Laxá I Adaldal—arguably Iceland's most famed Atlantic salmon river, celebrated for its large (by Icelandic standards) fish. Upstream of the Adaldal's storied beats—the Nes and Arnes—rests a much lesser known, but equally formidable fishery. The quarry here: brown trout.

"I have represented the salmon beats lower down on the river for many years," Peter McLeod began. "One year when I visited, the guides took me near the top of the river to show me the trout fishing. I didn't fish on that occasion, but it certainly whet my appetite. The guides had stories of double-digit wild browns coming from these waters, and they claimed that the fish fought harder than some of the salmon they hook in the lower river."

The Adaldal originates from Lake Myvatn in the north of Iceland, roughly forty-five minutes from the town of Akureyri. "Myvatn" means "midge" in English, and this moniker speaks to the abundance of insect life in the lake and in the river below. "It's a very high alkaline system," Peter continued. "This results in a tremendous amount of vegetation, which in turn supports abundant insect life . . . and trout. If you inspect a handful of weeds, it will be crawling with bugs." In its upper reaches, the Adaldal has a significant gradient, and is divided into two general sections: Myvatnssveit and Laxardal. "The Myvatnssveit is very braided, with white water, riffles, little pools, and runs," Peter added. "The Laxardal section is shallow and wide. It reminds me a bit of bonefishing in terms of the wading, as the river only comes up to your knees; you can walk right across it. The substrate is black lava sand, however, so it's quite difficult to sight-fish. Fortunately, you can often find the fish rising near the bank, feeding on little black *Simulium* and other bits and pieces of insect life floating by. The fish feed very hard, as there's a very short opportunity to eat in northern Iceland; by late August, it's already starting to get very cold."

OPPOSITE:

Known foremost for its Atlantic salmon fishing, the upper reaches of Laxá I Adaldal may comprise one of the world's finest wild brown trout fisheries.

Peter's first brown trout on the Upper Adaldal came on the Myvatnssveit beat, and the experience still resonates. "Bjarni was to be my guide, and he wanted to take us to one of his special spots. It was a blazing, sunny day, most idyllic. We never made it to the special spot. About 300 yards downstream from where we started, we came upon a group of fish sipping something small in the middle of the river. We couldn't figure out what the fish were taking, so I tied on a small black hopper. The water was nearly up to my chest and I couldn't wade in, so I had to cast nearly all the line I had to get a drift over the fish. Every so often, a fish would have a crack at it, but I didn't hook up. There was a larger fish at the head of the pack, and I started focusing on him. I drifted over the fish fifteen times, but he wouldn't take it. I figured I wasn't in the cue properly, so I watched him for a while to get a sense of how often he was coming up, and timed my next cast accordingly. I put the black hopper in, and the fish sucked it through the surface film, as gently as if it were a fingerling on an English chalk stream. When it felt the hook, it blasted out of the water like a missile. I usually play fish hard and leaned into the rod. The fish took off downriver like a scalded gazelle. My Hardy lightweight was making noises I'd never heard before— I thought it was going to explode. I couldn't palm the reel, so I ran downriver in pursuit. Eventually, we found some quieter water. Bjarni came up behind the fish with a little tennis racquet–shaped net. The fish was having none of this and tore across the river. I began pumping the rod and winding line in, as though I were fighting a tarpon. Bjarni eventually made a forehand volley of sorts and got part of the fish in the net, enough at least to admire and release it. The fish was 6 or 6.5 pounds. I'd never encountered such a powerful trout. I began thinking of them as Viking trout."

There are many ways to pursue the Adaldal's browns. "Many of the Icelanders fish streamers across and downstream," Peter said, "but I like to fish upstream with a dry fly or a nymph. Drys may be as small as size 16 or 18; with nymphs, I fish Sawyer style, without an indicator. During my last visit, fish averaged 3.5 to 4 pounds, with much larger fish present. I had one client there last year fishing near a set of rocks. He cast a size 12 nymph against the rocks and the fly stopped. He thought it was a rock . . . until the rock began swimming upstream and popped his 12-pound test leader. The fish are prolific, too. One friend fishing there early in the season landed thirty-eight in three days. There's so much water to explore. You just wander up and down the grass banks—there are no trees—and look for fish. The guides are direct and know the river well. Most do not guide full-time for a living due to the short season, but take time off from their regular jobs to guide for a month or two in the summer because it's their passion. On a given day, your guide might be head of a multinational corporation or the chief of police."

With its stark, dramatic scenery and wonderful fishing, Iceland has many appeals for angling travelers. For Peter, native cuisine is not among its attractions. "Icelanders have some truly—well, disgusting—foodstuffs. Local delicacies include lamb testicles, dried fish, and puffin, which is quite chewy. Most offensive of all was rotten shark—basically, shark meat that's rotted for three months, then cut and served. It smells of pure ammonia. I once asked a guide if he ever ate this stuff, and his reply was "No, it's only for tourists. Do you think we're nuts?!"

PETER MCLEOD has had a fly rod in his hand since he was seven years old and has dedicated his life to the pursuit of different species on the fly. After working in the tackle industry during school holidays in his midteens, he became a salmon fishing guide in Norway for Roxton Bailey Robinson until leaving university. Following a spell at Farlows of Pall Mall, he joined Frontiers International Travel in February 2000, where he remained for the next five years. He founded the fly-fishing travel company Aardvark McLeod at the beginning of 2005. During the past sixteen years he has fished extensively around the globe.

If You Go

▶ **Prime Time:** The season runs from early June to late August.

▶ **Getting There:** Fly to Reykjavik and then on to Akureyri. Both are served by Iceland Air (800-223-5500; www.icelandair.com) and partner airline Air Iceland.

▶ **Accommodations/Guides:** Guests stay at the two lodges that control the beats on the upper river—Raudholar and Hof. Both are represented through Aardvark McLeod (+44 1980 847 389; www.aardvarkmcleod.com).

▶ **Equipment:** A 6-weight with floating line will suffice. Local guides can provide the flies that are working when you visit.

MIÐFJARÐARÁ RIVER

RECOMMENDED BY April Vokey

"Though I grew up and live in the heart of steelhead country, I've always been fascinated by Atlantic salmon," April Vokey began. "I'm very passionate about fly tying, and the elegance of Atlantic salmon patterns have had a long appeal. I always felt a bit like a poseur, as I'd spend hours tying these wonderful patterns that were meant to be framed— Jock Scott's and the like—but had never had the opportunity to fish them. The lore of Atlantic salmon fishing, the places the fish swim, the flies—all is very romantic to me."

Imagine, then, when the e-mail came from Iceland as follows: "April, my name is Rafn Alfreðsson and I run a lodge on the River Miðfjarðará. We would like you to come to Iceland to put on a women's school in June next year, are you interested?" He didn't have to ask twice. "I remember that first e-mail very clearly," April added. "I couldn't pronounce his name, and I certainly couldn't pronounce the name of the river, but the rest of the text was clear. Given Iceland's incredible scenery and world-renowned Atlantic salmon fishing—of course I was interested!"

Among the upper shelf of Iceland's famed salmon rivers—the Adaldal, the Selá, and the Grimsa among them—the Miðfjarðará holds a special place, as much for its splendid intimacy and beauty as for its productivity. The Miðfjarðará system is roughly 120 miles due north of the capital city of Reykjavik, and the fishery includes four rivers—the main stem, the Austurá (including its celebrated canyon section), the Núpsá, and the Vesturá. Altogether, it encompasses more than 50 miles of fishable water, with more than two hundred pools of a wonderfully varied nature spread over just five beats, with only two rods per beat. MSWs (multisea winters) ranging from 10 to 18 pounds return to the system in the early weeks of the season, with fish in the 20-plus-pound class found each year. In mid-July, grilse join the mix; they run large, averaging 7 pounds. Catch rates can be

OPPOSITE:
*The Miðfjarðará
is an intimate
river. On some
sections, anglers'
best approach to
pooled-up fish
can be from above
the waterfalls.*

21

DESTINATION

97

phenomenal: in 2009, rods averaged four and a half fish a day. Double-digit days are quite conceivable!

Fishing on the Miðfjarðará is divided into daily six-hour sessions, from 7:00 A.M. to 1:00 P.M. and from 4:00 P.M. to 10:00 P.M. (Some anglers may choose to share sessions.) Thanks to the system's great clarity and adjoining topography, sight-fishing is possible on many of its pools. "There are mounds of rock everywhere and many waterfalls," April continued. "At some pools, we would sneak along on our hands and knees to try to spot fish before casting. Sometimes, I would find myself actually making casts from my stomach, above a waterfall. It was all dry line fishing with a single-hand rod. Oftentimes we fished our flies with a riffle hitch on the surface. If that didn't work, we'd go back through the run with a submerged pattern [like the unattractive yet highly efficient Francis fly]. Rather than swinging the fly, as you might with steelhead or Atlantic salmon in Quebec, anglers tend to strip the fly back. Some of the most exhilarating fishing of the week came as I cast from beside a waterfall. There's the sound of the rushing water, the spray that envelops you, and the knowledge that it's almost certain that there are fresh salmon stacked below the fall by the dozens. Fishing a spot like this, you try to present the fly where the churning white water softens out, where it's still white but not too fast. High-sticking a riffle-hitched fly through this water was very effective.

"I was taken with the Icelanders' tremendous sense of humor," April continued. "I imagine their wit goes back to their Viking ancestors—I love the story of how they arrived at the name of 'Iceland' to discourage other explorers from visiting. Icelanders love jokes and pranks. Before I arrived, Rafn told the ladies who worked at the lodge that I was paralyzed from the neck down, but could cast with my mouth. They were shocked when I showed up with working arms and legs. Every morning, when I went to put on my waders, there was something in my wading boots—rocks or raisins. One morning, I picked up my rod, and it was strung completely upside down. It's wonderful that they can laugh so, especially after the hard economic times they've been through." There are also interesting Icelandic practices that you may encounter along the river. "There's one tradition that says you should bite off the adipose fin of your first Atlantic salmon," April added. "Looking through some of my books on salmon fishing, I came upon photos of Icelandic children with bloody mouths, so I believe it's true—though since I'm a catch-and-release angler, I didn't indulge. There's another belief that says if you roll in the night dew naked on the solstice, you can attain everlasting youth. During my visit, a handful of my female students were in the hot tub one evening. It just so happened that it was the evening of the solstice. . . . laughing and hollering, they jumped out naked and rolled around on the dew-covered ground. They didn't realize that the men in the lodge happened to be at a nearby window and saw the whole event. I imagine it must have been quite a show."

Though April (and her students) found many fish in the course of her visit on the Miðfjarðará, it's the memory of her first Atlantic salmon that's burnished most brightly in her memory. "It was opening day of the season, and my guide, Jonni, and I were on Beat 1, on the main stem of the river below the junction of the Austurá and the Vesturá. I knew I was going to be the first person to fish the beat since the previous year, and my anticipation was tremendous. I missed a fish early on and watched Jonni land a beautiful specimen. At one point, I came up to a 'steelheady'-looking piece of water. I tied on a Collie Dog, and made a few casts, working line out and swinging the fly across the water, instead of stripping. After one cast, I lifted the rod to get the fly to skate a bit, and a huge mouth came up and smoked it. It turned out to be my biggest fish of the trip. The fish was chrome bright and spotted with sea lice, the surroundings were majestic—everything seemed too perfect to be true . . . it was just as I had always imagined."

APRIL VOKEY lives in British Columbia, Canada, and is a steelhead, salmon, and trout guide. She is a Federation of Fly Fishers Certified Casting Instructor, a fly-fishing columnist, and a lead angler for Fly Max Films. She can be found at www.flygal.ca.

If You Go

▶ **Prime Time:** The greatest concentration of MSWs are present late June opening and July 15. The greatest numbers of fish return between July 15 and late August.

▶ **Getting There:** The Miðfjarðará is near the town of Hvammstang, roughly three hours' drive north of Reykjavik, which is served by Iceland Air (800-223-5500; www.icelandair.com) and Iceland Express (866-512-8364; www.icelandexpress.com).

▶ **Accommodations/Outfitter:** Miðfjarðará Fishing and Hunting Destinations (354-824-6460; www.midfjardara.is) manages fishing and lodging on the Miðfjarðará.

▶ **Equipment:** A single-handed 6-, 7-, or 8-weight rod with floating line and 150 yards of backing will suffice. Small traditional wet flies, tube flies, and coneheads work well.

SOUTH FORK OF THE SNAKE

RECOMMENDED BY **Randy Berry**

"In my experience, the best western rivers for big trout have been the Missouri, the Yellowstone, and the South Fork," Randy Berry began. "The South Fork is also consistently ranked as one of the top dry-fly rivers in the west. You can take someone out on the South Fork who's never fished in their life and have them catching nice fish on a dry fly in five minutes. By the end of a day's float, they should have caught thirty trout, with an average size of 16.5 inches. That's how great the South Fork can be."

The South Fork of the Snake is a tailwater that flows some 60 miles in a northwesterly direction from the Palisades Reservoir in Wyoming to its confluence with the Henry's Fork, near Rexburg. In its course through Idaho's Swan Valley, the river is home to an average of 4,000 wild trout per mile, a blend of rainbows, browns, and cutthroat (only the cutts are endemic, though the rainbows and browns reproduce naturally). The river is divided into three general sections: the 12 miles below Palisades Dam, the roughly 24 miles of the Canyon section, and the last 28 miles between the Canyon and Henry's Fork. "The upper stretch below the dam is a little like a canal," Randy described. "We call it 'The Ditch,' though the fish are here and the mountain vistas are tremendous. As you come into the Canyon, cottonwoods and willows give way to junipers and pine trees dotting the canyon walls. There are seven ancient volcanoes along the South Fork, and you can see remains as you float along; the whole course of the river is in a caldera. When you leave the Canyon, the river winds through farmland, though you still have expansive views. The upper section has the highest concentration of rainbows. By the time you reach the lower section, the fishery is 80 percent brown trout.

"Whatever section you float, there's great fish habitat. Years ago, a guest put it this way: "Every time I look up, there's a place to cast for a fish. There just aren't any dead

OPPOSITE:
A beautiful South Fork cutthroat, the only trout species endemic to the river.

101

spots.' Another nice aspect of the South Fork is that you don't have to go out early. Thanks to the river's high elevation, bugs hatch later—mayflies, for example, don't come off until 10:30 or 11:00 A.M., unless it's been extremely warm. We always start out fishing four different flies: one angler will have two drys on, the other a dry and a dropper. As soon as someone has a take, we know what the fish are on, and we switch over. If you tie on a dry and dropper and don't get a fish in five minutes, you're doing something wrong. The fishing goes on all day. Many times we'll see 100- to 150-fish days for two anglers drifting. The best day I've had is 206 fish for two rods, all on drys. And on any given day, you're going to have a bigger fish—20 to 25 inches—hit. You may not catch them, but they'll hit."

The dry-fly fishing season on the South Fork begins in April, but thanks to high water and high elevation, things don't really get going consistently until early June. The first hatch of consequence are the green drakes, and the first major hatch of the year—and a favorite of many South Fork regulars—is the salmon fly emergence. "On average, the salmon flies will begin appearing on June 20, with a small variance depending on the snowpack," Randy continued. "It lasts until July 25 or perhaps 28. The big bugs [2 to 3 inches in length] bring up enormous fish—we've hooked fish of 12, 14, 16 pounds that we just can't land." Anglers don't need a lot of subtlety during the salmon fly season. Randy would advise you to leave the 3- and 4-weight rods at home. "We fish 6-weight rods with a Rio Clouser line, which has enough weight up front to turn over a big two fly rig—a 1/0 dry with a size 2 dropper. I like 12-pound test tippet. If you have the right fly on, the fish don't care about the thickness of your terminal gear. Some of the local guys use 20-pound tippet, as they hate to lose a fly! The fish will really gorge themselves, but they'll keep on hitting your fly. You'll bring in a 3- or 5-pound rainbow, and when you remove the fly, four or five real salmon flies will fall out of its mouth."

As the summer advances, the salmon flies are joined by golden stones. By the end of July, pale morning duns (the South Fork's most significant mayfly hatch) begin to steal the limelight from the big bugs. They're joined by caddis, which can blanket the water at times, resulting in outlandish surface activity. Late summer and early fall bring grasshoppers to the fore, and the hoppers are joined by another mayfly, mahogany duns. With the onset of cooler weather, the river's brown trout begin to bulk up as they anticipate spawning. Many anglers will couple frosty mornings with streamers. Throwing big Zonkers may wear down your casting arm, but it's worth the shot at a double-digit brown . . . or rainbow, as Randy described: "In December of 2007, our head guide, Tom Fenger, was fishing streamers with a client, John Short, on the South Fork. John was fighting a 6-pound brown when Tom yelled at him to come help him land a large fish. John broke off his 6-pounder and hurried over to Tom. Tom knew he had a big fish—he estimated it 12 pounds. When John arrived, Tom was about to beach the fish as neither of the men had a net. As Tom slid the 'bow through the shallow water onto the rocks, he and John were shocked at the size of this fish. They estimated the monster at 22.2 pounds."

Many come to this part of the world to take in its abundant wildlife, and the South Fork doesn't disappoint. "We see a lot deer on the river, and quite a few moose, with the odd black bear thrown in," Randy continued. "We've also been seeing more mountain lions. A few years back, I watched two lions take down a moose. The moose swam the river and didn't see the lions waiting in the brush. It took the lions two days to eat the moose down enough so they could move the carcass into the brush for future meals."

RANDY BERRY began guiding in 1959 at Teton Valley Lodge, when he was 5'2" (and thirteen years old). He has guided on the rivers of Montana, Wyoming, and Idaho for more than fifty years and today is the proprietor of Teton Valley Lodge.

If You Go

▶ **Prime Time:** The South Fork is open year-round, though good flows (and hatches) begin in late June and extend through September.

▶ **Getting There:** Driggs is base camp, and is best reached via Idaho Falls, which is served by Delta Airlines (800-221-1212; www.delta.com) and Horizon Air (800-252-7522; www.alaskaair.com).

▶ **Accommodations:** There are several lodges on the South Fork catering to anglers, including Teton Valley Lodge (800-455-1182; tetonvalleylodge.com) and South Fork Lodge (877-347-4735; www.southforklodge.com).

▶ **Guides/Outfitters:** A number of guides serve the South Fork, including, Teton Valley Lodge (800-455-1182; tetonvalleylodge.com) and South Fork Outfitters (800-483-2110; www.southforkoutfitters.com).

▶ **Equipment:** Locals opt for 6-weight rods for drys and nymphs, a 7-weight for streamers. The region's many fly shops can tell you what's working.

DESTINATION 22

SILVER CREEK

RECOMMENDED BY **Bob Unnasch**

Of the American West's great spring creeks, Silver Creek may hold the most mystique and the most potential to intimidate—even for Nature Conservancy scientist Bob Unnasch. "I grew up cutting my teeth on some of the fabled streams up in upstate New York—the Beaverkill, the Upper Delaware, the Little Beaverkill. When we weren't on the river, my dad and brother and I spent a lot of time talking about the famous streams that we'd have to fish one day—most of them out west. Silver Creek was near the top of the list. We'd often discuss it and look at pictures. It took much of my adult life to finally make it out."

Silver Creek emerges from the sagebrush steppe 25 miles southeast of Sun Valley, Idaho, in the shape of dozens of tiny spring-fed streams. By the time it reaches the Nature Conservancy Preserve near the Picabo Hills at the southern end of the Big Wood River Valley, it's a full-fledged river, a true oasis in this high-desert terrain. Thanks to its aquifer origins, Silver Creek's nutrient-abundant waters flow consistently cold and clear, sustaining lush aquatic vegetation and a plethora of bug life that in turn supports rich salmonid populations. When Ernest Hemingway first set eyes upon the river in the late 1930s, he saw endemic cutthroats dimpling the surface. Today, the cutts have been displaced by rainbow and brown trout, and a smattering of brookies, all introduced. (While nonnative species, Silver Creek's new denizens have been reproducing naturally for more than thirty years, along with mountain whitefish that are also endemic to the system. At present, the river's salmonid biomass seems to be tilting in the brown trout direction.)

Clear water, a maze of micro-currents, and hatches of subtle distinction—not too mention legions of anglers—make the trout of Silver Creek *rather particular* and have fostered the fishery's reputation as a pull-your-hair-out-to-get-a-take-among-all-the-rising-

OPPOSITE:
Silver Creek
bubbles up from
a series of springs,
and gurgles along
in the shadow of
the Picabo Hills.

DESTINATION **23**

trout venue. "My first few outings on Silver Creek completely fulfilled the river's reputation," Bob continued. "Now that I look back at it, it was like having a date with the prettiest girl in high school—the whole time you're on the date, you're too terrified to enjoy it! I did catch a few dinky fish those early trips, but I spent more time throwing every fly in my box to no avail. Nonetheless, when you're out there, you can feel the presence of your predecessors. That takes away some of the sting of the trout's rejections. And the river is still as beautiful and exciting and productive as when the Hemingways were casting with cane poles and catgut leaders seventy years ago."

While it was Ernest Hemingway who was invited to Idaho as part of the Sun Valley Company's efforts to promote the region as a summer-fall getaway (other celebrities who were courted include Gary Cooper), it was Ernest's son—Jack—who proved instrumental in preserving Silver Creek for generations to come. (The elder Hemingway preferred duck hunting to fly fishing, at least along Silver Creek.) Jack came to love Silver Creek, despite reports of fishless early outings, and when he became a commissioner with the Idaho Department of Fish and Game in the seventies, he was in a position to influence its future. He approached the Nature Conservancy in 1975 when 479 acres of land encompassing the upper stretches of the river went on the selling block, urging the organization to purchase it, lest it fall into the hands of vacation home developers. TNC made the initial purchase, and since then has acquired nearly 400 acres more; perhaps more significantly, TNC has also worked with many local landowners to place 10,000 more acres of riparian land into conservation easements. Though frequently irksome to newcomers and older hands alike, Bob Unnasch has found that Silver Creek, like any other river, begins to reveal itself over time. "What I've come to realize is that in some ways, it's an approachable, manageable-sized spring creek," he said. "Next to Silver Creek, a river like Henry's Fork is so gigantic, with so many feeding lanes, I find myself getting lost. On the flip side, other spring creeks are so tiny that you never have more than a leader and a few feet of line outside your rod tip—you're just dabbing flies. For me, Silver Creek is large enough where you can make an actual cast, small enough to make sense of. In that respect, it's reminiscent of the streams I grew up with. A wonderful thing about spring creeks is that there's almost always something happening from an insect perspective, and invariably the fish are on the feed. Of the many, many days I've been out on Silver Creek, I can only recall three or four when there was nothing happening. Most days you see fish flashing or rising—they're ready to play.

"Many people talk about the technical challenges on Silver Creek—the need for exact insect imitations. I find the greatest challenge to be of a predatory nature; that is, getting into the right place to make a cast without spooking the fish. If you walk carelessly along the river, the number of fish you flush out from the undercut banks is awe-inspiring. Even if you walk up to the river carefully in the early morning, you'll see wakes moving away from you. I've found the fish to be extremely line sensitive. If your line goes past a fish's field of vision, it's gone—and every fish in the vicinity is gone too. Long leaders are essential. I use a minimum of 12 feet, often 15 feet. Being invisible is key to success. Some people like to fish from float tubes in the Kirkpatrick Pond area and lower down (where the river deepens up). I think this approach can be productive, but much more so after dark. I believe these fish know what a float tube is all about."

Shy and selective as the trout of Silver Creek may be, there's always an exception to the rule, as Bob discovered one evening. "I took my brother and his son over to Silver Creek to fish the evening hatch," he recalled. "My brother is a little deliberate in assembling his gear, and I was on the water casting before he'd even closed the trunk. I made a few casts and hooked what seemed to be a big fish. It took a few good runs and broke me off. 'That's the game,' I thought, and continued fishing. My brother went into the river about 50 meters downstream. A few minutes later, he begins yelling. 'I've got a big one on, Robert. A really big fish! You have to come down here and get a picture.' I reeled up and hustled down river to get a photo. Examining the fish in his net, he said, 'Look—it's got two flies in its mouth!' I asked, 'Is it an elk-hair Caddis with a small dropper?' He said, 'Yes!' I replied, 'Well, that's my fish, then. You've got to take my picture.'

"It was a 21-inch brown. So much for the notion that if you nick a fish on Silver Creek, it's gone for days. My brother got his picture, and I got my flies back."

BOB UNNASCH is the director of science for the Nature Conservancy in Idaho. His responsibilities include providing research and monitoring guidance for TNC's Silver Creek Preserve. The conservancy is committed to protecting the entire Silver Creek Basin. Bob was introduced to fly fishing as a child by his dad, and has spent his life chasing sport fish around the Western Hemisphere. Growing up, he learned the art and science of trout fishing on the Beaverkill, the Upper Delaware, and their tributaries. He spent about ten years living on Long Island Sound, chasing bluefish and striped bass with a fly rod before relocating to Idaho and hanging up his 9-weight for a 3-weight.

DESTINATION **23**

If You Go

▶ **Prime Time:** Silver Creek is open for angling from Memorial Day through February. A favorite hatch for many anglers is the brown drake emergence, which occurs in early June. The Silver Creek Nature Preserve offers excellent public access; private land on the lower sections of the river requires anglers to float.

▶ **Getting There:** Twin Falls is the closest commercial airport and is served by Delta Airlines (800-221-1212; www.delta.com). From the state capital, Boise, it's a roughly two-hour drive.

▶ **Accommodations:** The Ketchum/Sun Valley area has many attractions for visitors, and the Sun Valley/Ketchum Chamber & Visitors Bureau (866-305-0408; www.visitsun valley.com) lists a range of accommodations.

▶ **Guides/Outfitters:** Several local guides can help unveil the secrets of Silver Creek, including Silver Creek Outfitters (800-732-5687; www.silver-creek.com) and Idaho Angling Services (208-788-9709; www.anglingservices.com).

▶ **Equipment:** A rod in the 4- to 6-weight class (the latter for windy conditions) outfitted with floating line will work for most situations. Consult local fly shops for what's hatching when you visit.

23

DESTINATION

WESTERN RAMGANGA RIVER

RECOMMENDED BY **Jeff Currier**

Jeff Currier's quest for mahseer began some years ago, with an e-mail to an Indian native named Misty Dhillon. "I had planned a two-month-long journey to India and Nepal," Jeff began, "and while it was not strictly a fishing trip, one of my main ambitions was to catch a giant mahseer on a fly. I'd heard that a fellow named Misty had been fly fishing for these creatures with some success, so I e-mailed him. I didn't hear back and went over blind. While it was an incredible adventure, I came up empty on the mahseer; on the Cauvery River in southern India where we sought them, it was primarily a bait fishery. The fish were too deep to effectively fly fish for.

"A few years later I was at a fly-fishing show in Sacramento, and a friend said that there was an Indian gentleman looking for me. As soon as I saw him, I knew it must be Misty. He said, 'Mr. Currier, I have long awaited a chance to meet you. If you ever wish to come back to India, I can make sure that you catch a Himalayan golden mahseer on a fly rod.' Remembering the bait bags and 20-ounce sinkers the guides had wanted me to use on the Cauvery, my immediate thought was 'No!' But eventually I changed my mind and made my way back."

Mahseer may be largely an unknown entity for most North American anglers, but British anglers know a bit about this game fish. A member of the carp family, mahseer fall into one of six or eight (depending on whom you speak to) species; the largest specimens approach 100 pounds (one of the largest caught on rod and reel eclipsed 120 pounds). During the days of the raj, Englishmen, pining for their salmon and sea trout streams at home, discovered the sporting potential of these large-scaled creatures, reputed to fight harder, pound for pound, than the salmon at home. (The scales of the mahseer are so large that one could be used as a luggage tag!) Interest in the mighty mahseer—at

least among westerners—waned during the postcolonial days. But in 1977, three Brits—Robert Howitt, Martin Clark, and Andrew Clark—inspired by earlier accounts of mahseer, set off to find them and immortalized their experience catching humpback mahseer on the Cauvery (using bait) in a book entitled *Quest for a Legendary Gamefish*. Ten years later, a documentary called *Casting for Gold* focused the spotlight on the Himalayan golden mahseer, which are more prone to take artificials than their southern cousins. Not long after this, these great fish, which are distributed throughout the waters of the Himalayas, attracted Misty's attention.

"I had been working as a rafting guide on rivers in the sub-Himalaya, and I had a powerful vision that placed me fly fishing for these fish on the rivers of northernmost India," Misty said. "It was all very clear in my mind, and I became very passionate about it, though I had no access to tackle. Eventually I got my hands on a Cabela's outfit and a fly-tying kit (made in India, I realized later!), and soon after I caught my first mahseer on the fly. Having a lodge and being able to lead visitors to the Himalayan golden mahseer is the fruition of my initial vision."

The Western Ramganga is one of the jewels of Misty's mahseer domain, a clear-running river that flows out of the lower Himalayas in the Indian state of Uttarakhand, coursing through a broad valley of tropical forests and elephant grass; a portion of the river adjoins the famed Corbett Tiger Reserve, home to some 164 tigers at last count. "It closely resembles a trout stream," Misty continued, "strewn with boulders, small rapids and riffles, and long tail-outs. It's quite a contrast to the big, muddy rivers in the south, and in some spots you can see mahseer everywhere. The Western Ramganga has many insects western anglers would recognize—hellgrammites, mayflies, stoneflies, crayfish—except they're much bigger. The smaller fish—below 10 pounds—can be fooled with insect patterns. The bigger fish—they can run up to 50 pounds—are primarily fish eaters. And they are very wary, akin to Atlantic salmon, steelhead, or permit. We fish them New Zealand style, walking the river until we spot a fish that's feeding. A 3- to 4-mile walk per day is typical. If an angler can experiment with different methods, from swinging a big streamer to upstream nymphing, he'll catch them."

Trout stream comparisons aside, you'll be very aware that you're far from home as you stalk mahseer along the Western Ramganga. Elephants are frequently seen (you'll sometimes walk their paths), and there are certain beats where you might encounter crocodiles. And then there are the tigers, as Jeff Currier relates. "After five days of the river

DESTINATION 24

OPPOSITE: The Western Ramganga runs mostly clear, and poses great opportunity for anglers hoping to land a golden mahseer on a fly . . . and perhaps spy a tiger en route.

being out of shape, it cleared up, and I had the chance to fish one of the least fished beats on the river. After getting an 8-pound fish in one pool, we came to another pool and I spied a larger fish, maybe 20 pounds, in a back eddy. I tied on a brown Morrish Sculpin and cast out. The fish I saw, which was distinctively black, sank out of view, but as the fly swung, a golden blob nailed it. For fifteen minutes, that fish kicked the living s— out of me, tearing up and down through several pools. I finally got it into the shallows, threw down my rod, and tailed it with two hands. It had to be the most beautiful fish I'd ever seen. When my guides came up, they were in awe. We weighed the mahseer—it was 27 pounds (a world record, as it turned out later). I did a half hitch around the fish's tail and tied it off to a log so it could revive itself; after a while, I flipped off the rope and it swam back into the pool.

"I realized that we had some miles to cover to get back to our rendezvous point with the Jeep, and I was eager to see sections of the river we had passed up. I noticed that the river had big bends, and that there was a massive trail, made by elephants, that made a straighter line upriver. I wasn't sure if it was safe; we'd seen a 14-foot python on one such trail earlier that had been stomped by elephants. But one of my guides said it was okay, so we started out, with me out in front. After a few minutes, I had this horrible feeling that something was watching me. There was dead silence, and the hairs were standing up on the back of my neck. Then I heard my guides behind me and continued on. After another fifteen minutes I had the same feeling, except worse. I thought it was elephants; I was on an elephant trail after all, and I was ready to be stomped. I froze, but there was nothing. The voices came up behind me, and I continued.

"I crossed the river following the trail and found myself in an old riverbed. There was a gravel bar to one side, a mountainside covered in jungle on the other. I got that feeling again. I stopped, and there was dead silence. Barking deer started going off all over. I looked up the hill, and behind a bush with bright green leaves, I spotted an eye looking right at me, just 40 feet away. I soon spotted the other eye, and then a head the size of a beach ball. Soon I could make out the body—the animal was focused on me, like any cat ready to pounce upon a mouse. I wanted to scream, but there was nothing in the tank. After what seemed like a lifetime, the motionless cat shifted its eyes ever so slightly up over my shoulder. I could hear my guides coming. At that moment, my voice returned: "Tiger! Tiger! Tiger!" The guides got to my side in time to see the tiger stand, 7 feet long and 5 feet tall. It turned sideways and slipped into the jungle."

DESTINATION 24

JEFF CURRIER worked at the Jack Dennis Fly Shop in Jackson, Wyoming, for twenty-three years, before striking out on his own. Jeff has taught fly fishing, guided fly fishers throughout Wyoming and Yellowstone National Park, and escorted anglers to fishing destinations throughout the world. To date, he has fly fished in more than forty-five countries and has caught 250 different species. He has made several television appearances including on *Fishing the West, Fly Fishing the World,* and *Ultimate Fly Fishing.* His articles, photographs, and artwork have graced the pages of magazines, catalogs, brochures, and books. Jeff is the author of *Currier's Quick and Easy Guide to Saltwater Fly Fishing* and *Currier's Quick and Easy Guide to Warmwater Fly Fishing* guide books. These books have become the standard introductions to saltwater and warmwater fly fishing. Jeff became a member of Fly Fishing Team USA in 1998 and competed in Zakopane, Poland. It was there that he led the team to one of its best-ever finishes with his staggering mix of 128 trout and grayling in just five sessions. In 2003 at the World Fly Fishing Championships in Spain, Jeff earned a bronze medal for individual performance among his international peers. Jeff is an accomplished watercolorist in addition to being a writer. Some of his artwork and published writing, as well as his blog, can be viewed at www.jeffcurrier.com.

24

DESTINATION

If You Go

▶ **Prime Time:** September and October have proven most consistent, as the fish are eager to eat after spawning. April is another good time to target mahseer.

▶ **Getting There:** Excursions to the Western Ramganga stage in New Delhi, which is served by most major international carriers.

▶ **Accommodation/Guides:** There's one game in town for fishing the Western Ramganga: Himalayan Outback (443-205-4342; www.himalayanoutback.com). Founded by Misty Dhillon, the camp has six huts and a dining area, all overlooking the river; tigers are frequently seen on the camp's grounds.

▶ **Equipment:** An 8- or 9-weight rod is ideal; bring floating line, as well as a line with interchangeable sink tips. Reels should be fitted with a minimum of 100 yards of 30-pound backing. Mahseer are subsurface feeders, so an assortment of nymphs and streamers will serve you best.

RIVER MOY

RECOMMENDED BY **Joe Healy**

For Joe Healy—a fly angler and Irish American by heritage—an opportunity to travel back to County Mayo and cast to Atlantic salmon represented a perfect fusion of passions, professional and personal.

"The Irish Tourism Board, along with a consortium called The Great Fishing Houses of Ireland, invited me to join them on a trip they'd assembled for journalists," Joe began. "Our itinerary was to fish at Lough Inagh in Connemara, a day on the sea in Clew Bay and then on to the River Moy in County Mayo. We'd stay at some wonderful lodges and be present during the traditional peak of the salmon season.

"As I came into the baggage claim in Dublin, I was met by concerned faces. Western Ireland was in the grips of what some had termed a fifty-year drought, and the fishing was going to be more difficult than usual—especially if we didn't see some rain. This was our experience at Lough Inagh [in Ireland, Atlantic salmon run into lakes and are targeted there as well as in the rivers]; the fish just didn't seem to be in. At Pontoon Bridge Hotel on Lough Conn, the winds came up, and we got blown out for possible fishing—though it finally started raining as well. Still, another day of fishing was lost. That night, I had dinner with Markus Müller, the fisheries information manager for the western region of Ireland. He was eager to see me and a German journalist named Franz Braunschläger have a good angling experience, and he'd arranged to help get us a beat on the River Moy the next day, in the town of Ballina—no small feat, considering that most beats on the Moy are leased a year in advance."

For salmon anglers, a beat on the River Moy is among the Emerald Isle's most coveted treasures. Runs on the Moy can reach upward of 60,000 fish (with roughly 75 percent of these fish grilse) on a good year, with rod-and-reel catch rates sometimes eclipsing 12,000

OPPOSITE:
The River Moy's
most productive
waters rest in
the center of the
town of Ballina.

115

fish. The main stem of the Moy runs 62 miles, entering the Atlantic at the town of Ballina, the self-titled "Salmon Capital of Ireland." There are runs where the backdrop might summon a stateside émigré's sentimental notions of idyllic County Mayo country-side, yet many of the river's most prolific (and hence most famous) runs are in decidedly less pastoral settings. In fact, the Moy's most sought-after beats are in downtown Ballina! (Thanks to a public works project on the river channel conducted in the 1960s, the Moy has a canal-like ambience through parts of its course. Many in the fishing community have expressed wonderment that salmon still return in such great numbers.)

"The following day we continued to the Mount Falcon Country House Hotel, where we'd be staying that night," Joe continued. "The Moy flows through the property, and there are ponds stocked with rainbows on the grounds and a castle-like lodge that dates back to 1876—all very pastoral. The winding road down to Ballina went through similar countryside. While I didn't think we'd be fishing in a setting like the big woods of mari-time Canada, I was a bit taken aback when we stopped in the center of town. Markus had arranged for me and Franz to fish the Weir Pool, the site of an old salmon weir and an upper subsection of the Ridge Pool, arguably one of the most famous of all Irish salmon beats. The river's banks were exposed, but there were old stone walls beyond on either side. In high water, it would be a quay. On one side of the river there's a promenade, on the other is the Western Fisheries Office and angler's hut, where visitors can drink coffee, smoke cigarettes, and watch anglers below.

"Though the setting was different from any other salmon stream I'd experienced, I was quickly removed from my urban surroundings once I began fishing the pool. The sound of the river tumbling out of the weir—that water music—brought me back to fly fishing, and I was focused on my immediate surroundings. I could feel the throb of his-tory, just being there. Salmon were jumping, and I fished the #14 Ally's Shrimp derivative and tube flies that Stuart Price, the fishing manager at Mount Falcon, had recommended. Sometimes I'd look up and see a family watching me from beyond the stone wall and fence along the river, but my attention was on the fishing. Stuart advised me to manage my casts and swings toward the end point of the swing, so my fly would arrive at a very specific piece of water in a particular way. I switched to some of my Maine landlocked salmon flies—Mickey Finns and Gray Ghosts—but beyond one tug, nothing was work-ing. At around 6:00 P.M., I thought I'd take some photos from a bridge above the run. Back out on the main street of Ballina, in my waders and wading boots, I came across the marketing manager for Mount Falcon, Shane Maloney, a lovely Irishman, raspy voiced, cigarette in hand, tweed jacket, and collared shirt. He said, 'I think I may have worked something out for you to fish tomorrow morning. One of our guests has invited you to take his beat on the Weir Pool. Be ready at 4:30.' I had been thinking that my shot at an Irish salmon was finished, but now I was going into overtime.

"That night, we got some rain. My mood was heightened by some Guinness, a fine meal, and the promise the rain held. Though the other journalists looked as though they were going to have a long night, I turned in early, with the promise that Shane would wake me up before our 4:30 date. I woke up at 4:30 with a jolt, thinking I'd missed my spot. I ran to the lodge and knocked on the immense oak doors until the night manager appeared. 'Can I help you?' he asked. 'I'm supposed to meet Shane,' I replied. 'He just came in,' the watchmen said, but went and got him. Shane rallied, and we were in town by 5:30. The angler that invited me to share the pool had gotten two fish and was thrilled. Before I stepped into the run, the head ghillie said I shouldn't be afraid to fish something a little larger than I'd fished the day before. I started with a hitched tube fly as the sun was beginning to rise behind the cathedral spire behind the Moy's Cathedral Pool. I switched to a Gray Ghost as I reached a deeper section of the run—the spot where I'd had a grab the previous day. On the third swing through, a fish took. I had a tingle up my spine—was this really happening?—I strip set and fought the fish slowly, as I didn't want it to run down into the next beat. I kept looking up at the fisheries office, but no one was watching . . . and no one was coming down with a net.

"I walked the fish to the shoreline—a bright 5-pound grilse—and cradled it in my hands. Still, no one looking. I had no camera, and wondered if anyone would believe that I'd caught it. I had tags and could've killed it, but couldn't do it . . . so I let it go and relished the fish slime on my hands.

"I retired the Gray Ghost for a shadow box that rests in my office, and tied on an Ally's Shrimp type fly Stuart had given me. I worked through the run a few more times, and then Shane appeared outside the hut, with his habitual cigarette. He pointed to his watch. We had to leave by 8:00, so my fishing would soon be done. As Shane was watching with the head ghillie, my line tightened again. Shane let out a whoop and twirled his hand—if he'd had a hat, I know he would have thrown it in the air. Soon I landed another grilse with the help of the ghillie, this one 6 or so pounds. Shane snapped a few photos with his cell phone to document the event. I was elated beyond words.

"Incredibly, Franz had told me the day before that he dreamed that I would catch two salmon on the Moy. It came to pass, and was an unforgettable experience."

JOE HEALY has had a rich career in journalism. He recently served as associate publisher of *Fly Rod & Reel* magazine, where he launched Fly Rod & Reel Books and started a Fly Fishing in Schools pilot program in Maine high schools. He was also an editor of *Outdoor Life* magazine in the early 1990s, and later served as editorial director of *American Angler, Fly Tyer,* and *Saltwater Fly Fishing* magazines. Joe was vice president and editor in chief of *Vermont* magazine from 2002 through 2007, and his book *Training a Young Pointer: How the Experts Developed My Bird Dog and Me* was published in 2005 by Stackpole Books. He also edited *Love Story of the Trout* (2010) and *In Hemingway's Meadow* (2009). His stories have appeared in *Ski Press, Boston Globe Sunday Magazine, Outdoor Life,* and other magazines. Joe's angling adventures have taken him from Ireland to Belize to Alaska and throughout the Rocky Mountains and coastal United States.

If You Go

▶ **Prime Time:** The Atlantic salmon season is open from February through September. Early summer is considered high season, though conditions are rain dependent.

▶ **Getting There:** The airport most convenient to County Mayo is in Knock, which is served from Dublin by Aer Arann (+353 818 210 210; www.aerarann.com) and London by Ryan Air (+353 1 248 0856; www.ryanair.com).

▶ **Accommodations:** The Great Fishing Houses of Ireland (www.irelandflyfishing.com) lists many lodges around County Mayo that cater to fly anglers, including Mount Falcon Country House Hotel (+353 96 74472; www.mountfalcon.com).

▶ **Guides/Outfitters:** To fish the best water on the Moy, you'll need to secure a beat. If your lodging can't arrange a beat, Salmon Ireland (www.salmon-ireland.com) can help. The Northwestern Regional Fisheries Board (+353 96 22788; www.northwestfisheries.ie) lists ghillies and leases the beats in Ballina.)

▶ **Equipment:** Anglers will generally fish a 7- or 8-weight rod; spey rods are used by many anglers. Floating line will generally suffice, though slow sinking tips will help get the fly down in some of the Moy's deeper pools. Ghillies will have a selection of local flies.

CASCO BAY

RECOMMENDED BY **Eric Wallace**

You're standing in the bow of an Action Craft skiff as your guide poles you along flats that seem to stretch for miles. A warm sun lights the way. Suddenly several V-wakes appear at one o'clock, and the guide calls out, "Drop it on 'em, 40 feet!" As you backcast, a lobster boat chugs into view, and Down East accents can be heard over the diesel engine.

You know you're not in Andros, but casting to skinny water stripers in Maine!

For most of the thousands of fly anglers who chase stripers up and down the eastern seaboard, flats and floating lines are not a significant part of the equation. It's all about structure, bulky flies, and sink tips. It was not much different for Eric Wallace . . . until the revelation came. "I was out with a client, poling along a section of shoreline in 4 or 5 feet of water. The angler set his rod on the gunnel, and as we ripped off over some flats to get to another spot, the rod fell off. I made careful note of where it went in—I knew there were clammers who worked the flat, and I wanted to find the rod before they did. On my next day off, I headed out to the flat. It was kind of mucky, but there was a mussel bar to the left where I could walk in. As I poked around for the rod, I noticed V-wakes off to the side—in bright sun, in 1.5 feet of water! The fish were coming on to this flat much earlier than I'd ever imagined. Learning how to catch them has consumed my angling for seven years."

Casco Bay stretches east and north some 220 square miles from Portland. While not quite "Down East" Maine in terms of location, Casco Bay has the rocky coastline and pine-dotted coves that define the state for many visitors. Though in the shadow of the Pine Tree State's largest city, Casco Bay has maintained much of its wild flavor; you're as likely to be accompanied by seals and porpoises as you move from flat to flat as you are other anglers. Several factors contribute to Casco Bay's fecundity as a striped bass fishery, despite being near the northern boundary of the species' range. The bay is fed by a

119

number of rivers—including the Presumpscot, the Androscoggin, and the New Meadows—which attract a host of forage fish, including herring, alewives, smelt, and eel. Beyond the river mouths, Casco Bay offers nearly 15,000 acres of mud and sand flats, with powerful 7- to 13-foot tides cycling water [and fresh bait] through the region throughout the day. "It's like a soup kitchen out there," Eric continued. "There are countless channels that run through the flats, and you can follow the tide changes for a long time. The stripers are social creatures, and one small group will take up with another until you have quite a group of fish assembled."

Fly fishing the flats of Casco Bay will be an adjustment for most striper fishermen accustomed to blind casting into rips or structure or dropping big Clousers into schools of fish busting bait. In fact, there may be more parallels to fishing Caribbean flats for bonefish or permit. For starters, anglers can leave the fast-sinking lines and foot-long baitfish patterns in the car—this is mostly a floating line game. Second, some anglers may need to adjust their expectations. "Some striper fishermen are numbers guys," Eric continued. "This kind of fishing is more challenging than other methods. Many times, you have to crack them right on the head, using a long leader and fairly light tippet—10- or 12-pound fluorocarbon. Sometimes the fish will spook, but other times they'll come right to it. I'll often use crab patterns instead of baitfish imitations, which also takes some adjustment. Anglers have to react quickly, as the window to make the presentation is brief. The 'Aha!' moment for people not accustomed to this type of fishing comes when the 17-foot boat is resting on some mud flats and they see stripers waking in next to no water. When they step onto the casting platform and make a throw, they suddenly understand the value of the flats, which they've generally ignored in terms of water."

One difference from Caribbean flats fishing that Eric pointed out—hooked stripers might sometimes run off the flat and wrap themselves around a lobster buoy. Chasing stripers on the flats is a special experience that's likely to burnish memories that will be shared with striper devotees and infrequent saltwater anglers alike. On a recent June day, Eric had his own chance to share the experience with two very special future anglers—his twin five-year-old girls. "I had done a morning guiding trip that had gone well, and by lunchtime, the weatherman was predicting that the temperature would hit 90—not terribly common for Maine. My wife suggested that we all head out to a nice beach we know of out on one of the islands in Casco Bay for a picnic. We motored out there, and after the family was settled, I poled over to a sand flat just a little ways from the beach. Pretty soon

OPPOSITE:
The site of a
poling flats
skiff screams
"Bahamas"—
until you spot
the pine trees in
the distance.

DESTINATION

26

I was sight-fishing to 30-inch stripers. I made seven casts with green crab patterns and hooked five fish, with a bright midday sun . . . in Maine! Better yet, my kids saw what was going on and got to watch. They see my boat parked in the driveway and know that I take people fishing, but I don't think they really understood what my job was about until this moment. Watching one of my girls running up the beach with a big smile as I landed one of those fish is my most treasured fishing memory."

CAPTAIN ERIC WALLACE is a fanatic saltwater fisherman and fly tier with twenty years of guiding behind him. His knowledge of the ocean ecosystem, his patience, enthusiasm, and teaching ability have won him accolades and features in magazines such as *Fly Fishing in Saltwaters, Gray's Sporting Journal, Saltwater Fly Fishing, On the Water,* and *Outdoor Life,* among many others. In 2010 he cohosted a TV show for a sportfishing magazine. He is a creative fly tier who has developed dozens of patterns for both Northeast saltwater and tropical flats fishing. His flies and techniques are featured in Dave Klausmeyer's *Patterns of the Pros.* Eric's experiences guiding in other areas of the country—including the Florida Keys, the Frying Pan River in Colorado, the Deschutes in Oregon, and fabled trout waters of Michigan—guarantee clients a memorable trip, regardless of experience level, conditions, or weather. He is on the pro staff of Scott Fly Rods and Hatch Fly Reels.

If You Go

▶ **Prime Time:** Stripers usually begin arriving in Casco Bay in early June, and the fishing remains strong through September.
▶ **Getting There:** Casco Bay adjoins Portland, Maine, which is served by many carriers.
▶ **Accommodations:** Eric recommends two properties in Freeport—Harraseeket Inn (800-342-6423; www.harraseeketinn.com) and Applewood Inn B&B (877-954-1358; www.applewoodusa.com).
▶ **Guides/Outfitters:** Eric Wallace (207-671-4330; www.coastalflyangler.com) pioneered "flats-style" striper fishing in Casco Bay.
▶ **Equipment:** An 8- or 9-weight rod outfitted with floating line and 150 yards of backing is ideal for the Casco Bay flats. Eric often uses crab patterns.

EAST CAPE

RECOMMENDED BY **Jad Donaldson**

At the outset of the award-winning short film *Running Down the Man*, angler Frank Smethurst offers the following summation:

> For the longest time, everybody has told my brother and I that you cannot catch a roosterfish on a fly. Here you are in this giant ocean, in big water, with a silly little fly rod, trying to catch this giant, pretty, brilliant fish. I mean, at some point you've got to say to yourself, "God you're really setting yourself up for this not to happen. . . ."

In the course of the film, Frank and his brother, William, go on to show that indeed it *can* be done. And their exploits—immortalized in YouTube clips that have taken the fly-fishing community by viral storm—have inspired others to go running down the man, including Jad Donaldson.

"I could spend all my life chasing permit, trevally, and roosterfish," Jad began. "To me, roosterfish are right in between the first two species—sometimes they can be pretty picky about eating a fly, other times they're just voracious. Though they're very fast and strong fighters, the greatest appeal to me for roosterfish is their appearance. Roosters are exotic, even sexy—and I don't often use that word to describe fish. As Frank Smethurst has said, they're the Liz Hurley of sport fish."

Roosterfish (*pappagallo* in Spanish) are a member of the jack family and indigenous to the inshore waters of the eastern Pacific, from Baja California to Costa Rica and Peru. Roosters can reach more than 4 feet in length and 100 pounds in weight, though 20-pound fish are more common. They are marked by one of the sportfishing world's most unique dorsal fins—a series of seven long spines, its namesake rooster comb. They

are exceedingly fast; watching a rooster close the 20 feet that rests between it and a fly will make you gasp! While roosters can be successfully pursued in deeper water off the Pacific coasts of mainland Mexico, Costa Rica, and Panama, it is on the East Cape of Baja California where roosters are in reach from the beach. This region—from Cabo Pulmo in the south to La Paz in the north—has become the epicenter for fly fishers seeking roosters. (It was also here on the calm waters of the Sea of Cortez that the Smethurst brothers filmed their famous assault.)

Baja California is a peninsula that extends 660 miles south from the California border, bounded on the east by the Sea of Cortez (which separates the peninsula from the rest of Mexico) and on the west by the Pacific. Baja is crisscrossed by four mountain ranges—Sierra Juárez, Sierra de San Pedro Mártir, Sierra de la Giganta, and Sierra de la Laguna—which divert the little moisture that flows over the peninsula, rendering the eastern side of Baja quite arid. The East Cape is a land of stark contrasts: Rugged brown mountains frame the background to the west as scrubland dotted with saguaro cactus stretches down to white beaches and the turquoise sea, with a cloudless, cerulean sky above. The party pleasure-seekers of Cabo San Lucas are far removed from the sleepy East Cape, where macadam roads often give way to gravel, and there's nary a Señor Frogs in sight.

Roosterfish are a sight to behold, striking enough to be an object of intense desire. But as in many amorous pursuits, the quest is frequently as engaging as the capture. For fly fishers on the East Cape, it means a day on the beach—walking, riding an ATV, or sitting—depending on your state of mind. "Fishing for roosters is all sight-fishing, and you need the sun high in the sky," said Bill White, who guides for roosters around Cabo Pulmo. "Most days don't start until 9:00, and the best fishing is usually over by 4:00—real banker's hours. One misconception that people who've never fished the East Cape have is that you always have to be running. Some people certainly will walk the beach, searching for fish on the move, but another option is to find a spot high on the beach with good visibility, and wait for the fish to come to you, sometimes with the aid of a teaser that's surf-cast into the blue water." Sometimes you'll see the fish coming out of the deeper water toward the beach from 50 or 60 yards away like dark torpedoes; other times, they'll appear out of the trough where waves break on the beach, just a few feet from shore. On a good day, you may see upward of fifty fish and have many shots, though anglers should be happy landing one good rooster in a day's outing. "The first time I went roosterfishing, I stepped out of the truck at the beach and asked the guy I was fishing with what the roosters look like," Jad

OPPOSITE: With its distinctive comblike dorsal fin, roosterfish are among the sport-fishing world's most aesthetically striking specimens.

DESTINATION

27

recalled. "He pointed to an incoming wave, and there was a black shape riding the crest of the wave, running sideways to the shore. I asked him what I should do, and his response was '*Get down there!*'"

Once the fish come in toward the beach to hunt or coral baitfish, the madness that is roosterfishing really begins. Roosters have excellent eyesight, and the fly—a 6- or 7-inch baitfish pattern flung on a 10-weight rod (many East Cape anglers prefer a fly called a Rasta created by Frank Smethurst)—needs to be presented a bit in front of the fish and then stripped aggressively. (To further speed the fly's motion, some anglers will step backward while stripping line, resulting in a nuanced dance step that might be called the Baja Soft Shoe.) Between the surf, the line that wants to tangle around your feet or rod butt, and the adrenaline rush of a large, aroused fish with its 'combs up' barreling in your direction, making the cast when a fish is coming right at you is a challenge. But when the fish turns right or left and you need to sprint ahead of it while keeping your line clear and not sinking that 2/0 hook into your scalp—then things really get interesting. Sometimes you'll only get one shot before the fish retreats to the deep; sometimes you'll get three or four, and find yourself sucking wind 150 yards up the beach from where you started. On this level, roosterfishing is the fly-fishing equivalent of the winter Olympics biathlon event, where competitors cross-country ski from target to target, trying to hit the bull's-eye.

"I've had fish take the fly 60 feet away, and I've had them take nearly at my feet," Jad added. "When I first started doing this, I thought I'd have to strip like a madman, but it's more about the fly accelerating, never slowing down. While they're willing to chase bait, they're not always dumb about it; though on one occasion, I had a fish going so fast that it beached itself!"

CAPTAIN JAD DONALDSON's professional piscatorial pursuits began in sixth grade when he wrote an essay stating his intentions to be a professional angler. Now, as a full-time fly-fishing guide (www.fishingwithjad.com) and instructor and with seventeen-plus years of experience, he has turned his ambitions into reality. With seasons of guiding in the Great Lakes and western Alaska under his belt, Jad now plies his trade in the fertile steelhead-filled waters of the Pacific Northwest as he has for the past ten years. Annual stints of guiding on the East Cape of Baja and hosting travelers to saltwater destinations have firmly placed Jad on the map of the fly-fishing world. He is employed as a guide and specialist by Kaufmann's Streamborn in Tigard, Oregon. His newest passion is the pursuit of albacore tuna on the fly rod off the Oregon coast and plans for a saltwater sportsfishing operation are in the works. He resides in Portland, Oregon, and thanks his wife, Sarah, for all of her support.

| If You Go |

► **Prime Time:** Roosterfishing heats up with the temperature, so May through July tend to be best.

► **Getting There:** Most visitors fly into the Los Cabos International Airport, which is served by many North American carriers. The East Cape is roughly an hour's drive from the airport.

► **Accommodations:** Pappagallo (www.cabopulmoecopalapa.com) offers palapa-style lodging on the beach in Cabo Pulmo and can provide guide services. Hotel Punta Colorada (877-777-8862; www.vanwormerresorts.com) offers more upscale accommodations, also on prime rooster beaches.

► **Guides/Outfitters:** A number of guides lead fly fishers to roosters on the East Cape, both from the beach and from *pangas* just off the beach. These include Bill White (www.trophyflyfishing.com), Baja Flyfishing (www.bajaflyfish.com), and Bay Anglers (www.bayanglers.com). Jad Donaldson (www.opportunityfishing.com) also leads rooster trips during the prime season.

► **Equipment:** A 10-weight rod fitted with a clear intermediate "slime line" is ideal for beach fishing. Your reel should have 400 yards of backing; you can't chase the roosters once they take off into the ocean! The favored Rasta flies are available once you arrive.

DESTINATION

27

COSTA MAYA

RECOMMENDED BY **Bill Marts**

Costa Maya rests on the southern edge of Mexico's Yucatán coastline, stretching from Bahia del Espiritu Santo in the north to Chetumal Bay (and Belize) in the south. It's a sleepy region, a far cry from the hubbub of the Riviera Maya below Cancún. (One has the sense that the moniker "Costa Maya" was the creation of hopeful developers; growth may still come, but it hasn't yet!) Both Bahia del Espiritu Santo and Chetumal Bay boast abundant bonefish opportunities, as well as permit, snook, and tarpon—and both see less fishing pressure than better known Ascension Bay to the north. While the off-the-beaten-path flats of Costa Maya are certainly an attraction, a unique angling proposition in this region is the chance to jump juvenile tarpon in a series of salt/brackish water lakes that rest anywhere from one hundred yards to several miles inland from the Caribbean . . . the tarpon lakes of Costa Maya.

"In my years of working in the fly-fishing travel business, I've done a lot of business with a fellow named Alejandro Vega, whose nickname is Sand Flea," Bill began. "Sand Flea travels all around the Yucatán researching new fishing destinations and teaching local fisherman how to fly fish so they might someday guide. I joined Sand Flea on one of these exploratory trips, and we fished the flats of Chetumal Bay near the village of Xcalak. There was hardly anyone there, and the fishing was quite good, with lots of bonefish and permit. We drove north along the coast, and the angling continued to be productive, and I thought this was a place worth visiting again.

"On my next visit, some guys mentioned that there was a lake that had tarpon and crocodiles in it. It wasn't the kind of lake you could just drive up to, it was way back in the mangroves. It took a while to figure out where the lake was. Once we did, we rented a 12-foot fiberglass boat and hacked our way 400 yards into the lake. It took four hours to make it in, with our guide hacking through the mangroves and Sand Flea and me carrying the boat. When we reached it, we saw fish rolling, and soon hooked up with some baby tarpon. Their backs were black like the water, and they seemed to have bigger eyes. On the way out we cracked the boat, trying to wedge it through the mangroves."

The mangrove-enshrouded lakes and their inhabitants—snook, barracuda, and snapper, in addition to the tarpon—are a phenomenon peculiar to the state of Quintana Roo on the eastern side of the Yucatán Peninsula. Here, cenotes (pronounced "say-no-tays") punctuate the limestone strata, granting access to underground rivers and caverns. Near the town of Majahual, cenotes connect roughly a dozen lakes to the Caribbean, allowing salt water (and a host of its denizens) to pass freely back and forth. The lakes themselves are shallow, seldom exceeding depths of 4 to 6 feet; brimming with baitfish and other feed, they provide an ideal nursery for young tarpon. The Mayan people revered cenotes, viewing them as portals to a spiritual world below the earth. Fly anglers who've had the chance to visit the lakes profess a similar reverence. The reason is simple—the tarpon here are contained in a relatively finite space, providing visitors multiple opportunities to jump fish. Since access is limited to a small group of permit holders, the fish see very few flies, and thus remain aggressive toward streamers, a deer-hair bug called a Snookeroo, and even poppers.

Aggressive may be a gross understatement. While these juvenile tarpon are a fraction of the size of the hundred-plus-pound behemoths that patrol the flats and reefs of the Caribbean, they lack none of their elders' penchant for violent takes, which telegraph through an 8-weight fly rod like a roundhouse right to the temple. If you're not jolted into the present by a tarpon's take, its first jump—generally within one to three seconds of the take—will put you in a panic mode. The visceral fury of that leap, with the sun glinting off the fish's large silver scales as if it were a spiraling chrome bumper instead of the largest member of the herring family, sparks an unfortunate Pavlovian response from unschooled tarpon anglers: You immediately lift the rod, which 99 percent of the time will terminate your connection to the tarpon. (First-timers will claim that they're reverting to trout fishing techniques; it's been conjectured that the rod lifting is instead a fear response, an attempt on the angler's part to shield himself or herself from the projectile outside the boat!)

Anglers wishing to experience the baby tarpon of Costa Maya needn't chop their way into the lakes or bear a boat upon their shoulders—though accessing these waters still entails a sense of adventure. "Paradise Lodge has permits to fish the lakes, and they've carved little pathways into the lakes that are just big enough to accommodate a panga," Bill continued. "Guides back a trailer up to the entrance and bring the boat in. There's a thrill going in as the guide poles you through the mangroves—or, in some cases, as you pull your way through. There are mangrove crabs and other creepy crawlies scuttling around on the branches, and the cries of egrets and herons. When you come out, there's the brilliant reflection of the lake, and you're the only one there. You have the feeling that you've discovered the place." Fly fishing for tarpon on the cenote-fed lakes can be something of an endurance contest. There's a lot of blind casting with large flies to the mangrove shoreline, sometimes battling a significant wind. The closer your fly is to the mangroves the better, as the fish often tuck far beneath the foliage; it's not uncommon to hear fish splashing about in a foot or so of water under the mangroves. Casts to the edge or below the mangroves will occasionally draw a fish out from the shadows, but as often as not, you'll be poling over to the shoreline to retrieve your fly from the trees. Still, if you're not landing in the mangroves now and again, you're probably not fishing as effectively as you could be. Depending on water clarity, wind, and cloud cover, you may have the chance to sight cast to fish. Clear skies with a slight chop on the water is perfect.

"As much fun as the lakes are, the proximity of the flats to the north and south add another dimension to your week of fishing," Bill added. "Bahia del Espiritu Santo is very untouched. There's little commercial fishing and hardly any recreational pressure. In my experience, the bonefish there are bigger than other Yucatán fish. There are some approaching double digits.

"And if the wind comes up, you can always head back to the lakes. At so many lodges, you're out of luck if the wind is whipping. On the lakes, in anything less than a hurricane, there's always a leeside."

BILL MARTS is the saltwater travel sales specialist at The Fly Shop (www.theflyshop.com) in Redding, California. He has spent sixteen years in specialty fly-fishing travel sales, thirty-four years in specialty fly-fishing retail sales, and was the director of Sage Fly Fishing Clinics for three years. He is an author, lecturer, photographer, casting instructor, fly tier, and a spey-casting specialist. Bill has fished extensively in Alaska, Australia, Tahiti, Venezuela, Costa Rica, the Florida Keys, the South Pacific, Mexico, the Bahamas, Belize, Canada, and nearly every steelhead river in the Pacific Northwest.

▶ **Prime Time:** Fishing can be good throughout the year, but June through August tend to offer the best fishing . . . though it may be too warm for some. The chance of a cold front can make late fall and early winter a roll of the dice.

▶ **Getting There:** The town of Majahual, at the heart of Costa Maya, is roughly five hours south of Cancún, which is served by most major carriers. Lodge operators provide shuttle service.

▶ **Accommodations/Guides:** While there are some freelance guides in the Majahual/Xcalak region, your best bet for access to the tarpon lakes and Bahia del Espiritu Santo is Paradise Lodge, which can be booked through The Fly Shop (800-669-3474; www.fly fishingtravel). Most guests visit for seven nights/six days of fishing.

▶ **Equipment:** You'll need at least two rods to cover angling possibilities, perhaps more. An 8-weight will cover baby tarpon and bonefish, and a 9-weight is good for permit; a 10-weight is nice to have in case you come upon a bigger tarpon; all should be outfitted with tropical saltwater floating lines and 200 yards of backing. The Fly Shop can provide a list of recommended flies.

DESTINATION

28

BIG HOLE RIVER

RECOMMENDED BY **Denise Schreiber**

When the carrel-corseted office worker in Manhattan or Pittsburgh lets her fancies drift beyond the work-flow diagrams pasted about her cube to the trout streams of the mind, chances are good they drift to the west. To the Rockies. To Montana. For Denise Schreiber, they come to rest in the vicinity of the Big Hole Valley.

"The Big Hole region exudes the essence of the West," Denise began, "from the beauty of the setting—some of the most magnificent scenery I've seen in the Rockies—to even the names of landmarks, like the Pioneer Mountains. I also like the fact that the Big Hole River [and the other streams in the region] are not as pressured as some of the other 'big name' rivers like the Madison, the Bighorn and the Yellowstone, where it can be like bumper boats during high season. Even getting to the Big Hole is an adventure. Coming from the east might necessitate waking up in the middle of the night and end up taking two or three flights to reach Butte by the afternoon. It's just part of the journey, and people are happy to do it."

Unmitigated by impoundments and rich in "Big Sky" scenery and wild trout, the Big Hole fulfills the promise that the phrase "Montana trout fishing" holds out. It begins in the Beaverhead Mountains near the Idaho border and flows 155 miles north, east, and then south before emptying into the Jefferson River at the burg of Twin Bridges. The Big Hole is a study in contrasts, running through high mountain country, sprawling valleys, and rugged canyons. It also provides great salmonid diversity—brook trout and grayling in the upper river, trophy browns and rainbows in the mid and lower river, with a few cutthroat scattered throughout. "The Big Hole is special vis-à-vis other great Montana rivers in that it's still undeveloped," offered Craig Fellin, longtime guide and proprietor of the Big Hole River Lodge. "This is largely because of the ranchers in the valley. They're

OPPOSITE:
The Big Hole fulfills most visitors' expectations of a Montana trout stream: great scenery and great fish.

DESTINATION

29

key to the future of the watershed. Some people think that there would be more water in the river if the ranchers weren't operating, but the reality is, if you had housing developments along the river, there would be irreversible change. So far, the ranchers are hanging in there and passing the land along to the next generation."

Much of the fishing on the Big Hole is done from a driftboat, and visitors will want to leave enough time to experience the river in all its diversity through a few different floats. "It's almost like you're on a different river each day," Craig continued. "You have slower pools up above, a mix of riffles and pools in the middle, and faster water in the canyon section toward the bottom reaches. Here there are lots of undercut banks and fallen cottonwood trees, which make great lies for bigger brown trout. One of the things I enjoy about fishing the Big Hole is that if you're patient with a dry fly, you'll be rewarded. We use attractor patterns a lot. Even if there are no bugs on the water, you can get fish on top if your presentation is good." Big Hole trout have good reason to be looking up. Midges begin to emerge as ice gives way to open water in early spring, providing a warm-up (for trout and anglers) for the big entrée fare of salmon flies in June. Summer brings caddis and pale morning duns to the fore with grasshoppers coming online in August. As the air cools in September, Blue-Wing Olives become a focal point for dry-fly aficionados, though anglers shooting for big browns will go low with big streamers, especially in the lower river.

As anyone who's traveled to southwestern Montana knows, you can throw a stone in almost any direction and find good—if not great—trout water. "During visits to the Big Hole region, I've fished the upper sections of Rock Creek, which is in some ways like a miniature Big Hole," Denise said, "and I've also fished the Upper Bitterroot. Craig Fellin has access to a section of the Lower Beaverhead where the fall hopper fishing can be sensational. There's also 3 miles of McCoy's Spring Creek that he leases. It's a classic, technical spring creek fishery where you're stalking fish, sometimes casting from your knees. The browns and rainbows in McCoy's average 18 inches and go to 25 inches. Lastly, you can horse pack in to high lakes around the valley and cast to huge cutthroat that seldom see a fly."

A key ingredient in a memorable Montana trout fishing experience for Denise is the lodge. More than just a bed and a meal, the feeling of a lodge can set the tenor for the whole adventure. "To me, the Big Hole Lodge is one of the most classic fly-fishing lodges I've ever visited," Denise enthused. "When you arrive in Butte, the first person you see is either Craig Fellin or his son, Wade. Having the lodge owner greet you is a great way to begin a trip, and speaks to the Fellins' passion for what they do. The lodge is small, with a maximum of twelve guests. Craig could easily build another facility and fill it up, but he doesn't want to hurt the experience. At a lodge like this, people who don't know each other at the beginning of the week will book the same week in following years so they can see each other again and develop friendships that last a lifetime. The cabins have beautiful views of a meadow [where moose are frequent visitors] and the Wise River [which holds cutthroat and big migratory browns in the fall]. Another great aspect of the Big Hole Lodge is the tenure of the guides. These aren't kids just out of school, they're seasoned, grizzled guys who've spent decades on the river."

DENISE SCHREIBER is a sales specialist for Frontiers (www.frontierstravel.com), responsible for the American West, Belize, and Los Cabos, Mexico. Her angling travels have taken her throughout the Rocky Mountains, and she has cast to permit, bonefish, and tarpon in Belize and sat in a fighting chair on a 31-foot Bertram in Los Cabos with a marlin on her line. "Not a bad day at the office!" Denise likes to say.

If You Go

▶ **Prime Time:** The Big Hole is open to fishing from late May through November. Late June through September offers the most reliable river flows and hatches.

▶ **Getting There:** The closest airport is in Butte, Montana, which is served by Delta Airlines (800-221-1212; www.delta.com).

▶ **Accommodations:** The Big Hole Lodge (406-832-3252; www.flyfishinglodge.com) has earned an excellent reputation over more than twenty-five years of operation. The Montana Office of Tourism (800-847-4868; www.visitmt.com) lists other accommodations around Wise River in the heart of the Big Hole Valley.

▶ **Guides/Outfitters:** Guides are provided at Big Hole Lodge. Other options include the Complete Fly Fisher (866-832-3175; www.completeflyfisher.com) and Troutfitters (406-832-3212; www.bigholetroutfitters.com).

▶ **Equipment:** A 5-weight rod with floating line will suffice for most situations on the Big Hole. Anglers fishing smaller creeks might bring along a 3- or 4-weight as well.

DESTINATION

29

MIRAMICHI RIVER

RECOMMENDED BY **Bill Taylor**

There is probably no river more synonymous with Atlantic salmon angling than New Brunswick's Miramichi. Nineteenth-century riverside settlers wrote in their journals of being unable to sleep, thanks to the all-night splashing of returning fish. Biologists believe that as many as 1,000,000 fish may have once returned to the river; today, returning grilse (salmon that spend one winter at sea) and MSWs number from 50,000 to 100,000. While a shadow of its past former fecundity, this run still comprises one of the largest Atlantic salmon populations in the world; it's no wonder that the Miramichi kicks out nearly half of the rod-caught salmon in North America!

Some wags will tell you that the Miramichi is a short salmon river, just a handful of miles in its main stem where the Northwest and Southwest branches come together near the towns of Chatham and Newcastle. There is truth to this; the Miramichi as a fishery is really more a vast river system than one river, draining nearly a quarter of New Brunswick, and comprising some 700 miles of angling water. "The Miramichi has something for every Atlantic salmon angler," Bill Taylor opined. "You have public water, private water, old established camps and lodges. There's a big, wide river in the lower stretches that are often fished with 26-foot-square stem canoes. Some of the tributaries [there are more than a dozen] are quite intimate, and they're all very different. In fact, some of the tributaries—the Cains, Dungaron, Little Southwest, Renous, and Sevogle, to name a few—are great salmon rivers unto themselves, with returns of 2,000 to 5,000 fish. The fact that you have all of these different tribs getting different runs of fish means that there's potential for good fishing the whole season. Some people will visit the same camp each year and fish the same 3- or 5-mile section, and have a great experience. I've been lucky enough to fish many sections of this vast watershed. There's a lot to get to know and fall in love with."

OPPOSITE:
Fall colors grace
the Miramichi
in the late season
when the big
fish arrive.

DESTINATION

30

Fishing on the Miramichi falls into four basic seasons: In the early spring, anglers can cast to spring salmon (fish that have spawned the previous fall and are returning to the salt) with sink tips or sinking lines. You have the potential to catch good numbers of fish this way, though this fishery will hold little interest for anglers seeking sea-bright fish. The first wave of fresh fish generally arrives by early June, and pods of this first run of fish are still entering the river into mid-July. This first run comprises the greatest number of MSWs to enter the river. This run is followed by a significant influx of grilse. The season's last run begins in September and carries on until the season's conclusion. The fall run generally produces the biggest fish of the season, with specimens sometimes reaching into the 30-pound range and larger.

Beyond the better than average odds of hooking up with a salmon, one of the lures of the Miramichi is the opportunity to be immersed in the rich lore of the sport. Sportsmen have been plying its waters since 1850; the first private angling club, the Miramichi Fish and Game Club, was established in 1893. One part of the tradition is manifested in the flesh by the river's seasoned guides. "Many of the guides grew up on the river," Bill explained, "and their fathers worked at fishing camps and their grand-fathers worked at fishing camps. One such fellow is Ernest Long, who's been working at Wilson's Sporting Camps for more than seventy years. Even when he was a paratrooper in WWII, he never missed a season. I believe that Ernest knows more about why a salmon takes a fly than the salmon themselves know. Guides like Ernest also know exactly where the fish are most likely to be caught. It's not just knowing where the fish might hold, but knowing what sections of the pool where the takers are likely to be. There might be fifty or a hundred fish in a given pool, but it's the fish that's 3 feet below that rock on river right that's going to take. The Miramichi has many guides with the sort of knowledge that Ernest brings to the water." (*Note:* New Brunswick's regulations and access rites can seem a bit Byzantine to the uninitiated. The bottom line is, if you are not a New Brunswick resident, you need to retain a local guide to fish, and your guide will be able to lead you to accessible public waters . . . or outline options for secur-ing access to private or Crown-owned water. If you fish through a lodge, you'll have access to water that its proprietors own or have leased; unless you have good local con-nections, this is the best way to go!)

Another touchstone of the Miramichi experience is the chance to drift a Bomber over fish resting in one of the system's countless pools. Most credit the Miramichi for the birth of dry-fly fishing for Atlantic salmon. As Paul Marriner recounts in *River Journal: Miramichi*, an avid angler named Reverend Elmer Smith tossed a cigar butt into the river one day, only to see a fish rise from the depths to engulf the detritus moments later. The good reverend, perhaps sensing he'd received a divine revelation, hurried home and fashioned an imitation of his smoke from deer hair, which came to be known as the Bomber. "Bombers are most effective when they are dead-drifted on the Miramichi, just as you would a trout fly." Bill added. "The salmon here rarely take a skated fly, though they hit them with gusto on other rivers. When the water temperature gets to 64 or 65 degrees, you're into ideal dry-fly time. If you can only get away a few days a year, late June and early July can be a magic time."

A special river can bring a special zest to life. For Bill Taylor, the Miramichi has helped sustain life itself. "I went through a tough battle with cancer a few years back. I spent two months in the hospital and had six months of chemotherapy and radiation, which almost killed me, literally. Those nights in the hospital were lonely and painful. I'd close my eyes and think of what my good friend [the writer] Charles Gaines told me: 'When it's really rough, close your eyes and think about your most favorite place in the world.' For me, it was the Miramichi, and the time I spent there with my family and friends, watching my kids catching their first trout and salmon, seeing bull moose, listening to a pack of coyotes howl at a full moon, learning about catch and release, and sharing stories around the campfire at night."

BILL TAYLOR has been on the staff of the Saint Andrews–based Atlantic Salmon Federation since 1988. In 1995 he became president and chief executive officer. The Atlantic Salmon Federation is an international conservation organization dedicated to conserving the world's wild Atlantic salmon and their environment. He took up fly fishing when he was thirteen, and began Atlantic salmon fishing as soon as he secured his driver's license. Bill regularly fishes the Miramichi in New Brunswick, and has also fished the salmon rivers of Labrador, Newfoundland, Nova Scotia, Russia, and the Gaspé Peninsula in Quebec. He lives in Saint Andrews, New Brunswick, with his wife and daughters.

DESTINATION

30

If You Go

▶ **Prime Time:** The first wave of MSWs arrives from mid-June through July. The second wave hits from mid-September through October. In May, you can fish for spawned-out fish that are returning to the Atlantic.

▶ **Getting There:** Fredericton has the closest commercial airport, and is served by Air Canada (888-247-2262; www.aircanada.com) from Toronto and Montreal.

▶ **Accommodations/Outfitters:** Bill Taylor's favorite lodge on the river is Wilson's Sporting Camps (877-365-7962; www.wilsonscamps.nb.ca). You'll find a list of other lodges at the W.W. Doak website (www.wwdoak.com); the store, in Doaktown, has all the flies and other fishing supplies you need. While in Doaktown, you'll want to visit the Atlantic Salmon Museum (www.atlanticsalmonmuseum.com).

▶ **Equipment:** Anglers will use anything from a 7-weight to a 10-weight rod; most can cover the water well with a single-handed outfit. Floating line will suffice most of the year, though in the early season a sink tip might come in handy; 150–200 yards of backing should suffice. You'll want to have a few Bombers in your fly box; your guide will undoubtedly have his favorites.

DESTINATION

30

HAWKE RIVER

RECOMMENDED BY **Mike Crosby**

"I was surfing around on the Internet—I don't even recall what I was searching for—and came across an ad for a salmon lodge that was for sale in Labrador," Mike Crosby recalled. "I've fished for Atlantic salmon in Labrador for more than thirty years and believe it's one of the last great places for salmon angling, and was intrigued. So much of Newfoundland and Labrador is still inaccessible by road, there are great runs of fish, and a finite amount of anglers. To me, it's one of the most remarkable places to fish for salmon in North America. When I called the number listed, the fellow said that the lodge was on the Hawke River. I'd never heard of the Hawke River. I called some of the salmon anglers I know who like to visit Labrador, and they'd never heard of the Hawke River either. This blew me away! I had to get out a detailed map to find out where it was in relation to the rivers I knew. But some associates and I were interested. "We were under a time constraint to make a decision about purchasing the lodge, and the owner supplied names and numbers of previous clients. We contacted a half dozen anglers, and they had only good reports for the fishing. Based on those reports, we made an offer on the lodge without ever seeing it."

Labrador comprises what is arguably the wildest country left in eastern Canada. The mainland portion of the province of Newfoundland and Labrador is characterized by tundra in the north, small fishing villages in the coastal south, and thick spruce and tamarack forests in the interior, the provenance of moose, black bear, and herds of migrating caribou. Lee Wulff further burnished a stellar fishing reputation—and helped publicize the sporting possibilities of this remote country—with his bush plane expeditions around Labrador in his trusty Piper Cub, forever in search of new Atlantic salmon fisheries. (These adventures are chronicled in his wonderful book, *Bush Pilot Angler*.) The

Hawke is situated near the easternmost edge of Labrador, just north of the Strait of Belle Isle, which separates Newfoundland from the mainland.

"Part of the lure of a trip to fish the Hawke is the process of getting to Labrador," Mike continued. "You have to work to get there—first to Labrador, then to Charlottetown, then a twenty-minute bush plane ride from a lake near Charlottetown into camp. The first thing that caught me was the wildness of the place. Some great salmon rivers flow through communities, and can't help but be blemished by their detritus. There's nothing on the Hawke beyond our camp—no garbage, no cigarettes, no nothing. The Hawke is one of those places you can go and fish in seclusion, even though it's a public watershed. And there's still great potential for adventure. On one of my earlier visits, we traveled up the Hawke about an hour to a place called the Black Bear Pool with the former owner. We fished the pool and landed a few salmon. I asked the fellow where the next pool upstream was. He said, 'I don't know, I've never been further upstream. We've always caught all the fish we wanted here and below.' Making my way upriver, I was fairly certain that I was fishing water that had never seen a fly."

The lower Hawke River is formed by the confluence of the Northwest Feeder and upper Hawke River. Both are medium-size in stature, and both see similar runs of MSWs (multisea winters) and grilse, with a majority of fish being grilse, as is typical in Labrador. MSWs ranging from 8 to 20 pounds enter the river in late June–early July, followed by grilse. The grilse make their presence known by frequent jumps and rolls.

"The two rivers provide a great diversity of salmon water," Mike described. "There are stretches of more difficult water for the seasoned angler, pools that are well suited to dry flies, and a number of places where an inexperienced angler can catch salmon with some regularity. Fathers will bring their kids up to catch their first salmon—if a child can get 15 or 20 feet of line out, they can get a fish."

Mike painted a general picture of the angling program: "The lodge accommodates eight anglers a week. The floatplane lands on the river and ties up right in front of camp, which is less than 4 miles from the salt. There's a long home pool just upstream where the Northwest Feeder enters the Hawke. One twosome will fish that water, another group will head upstream by boat on the Northwest Feeder. They'll portage a set of falls, jump in another boat, and head upriver another fifteen minutes, where another pool awaits. Within a half hour's walk upriver, there are four or five more pools, and a little camp where anglers can take lunch or opt to stay overnight. The other four anglers will head up the Hawke by boat. Two will fish a series of pools called Dawn's Pool, the second set of anglers will continue upstream to an ATV that will take them upriver to the Black Bear Pool—and beyond, if they wish. There's a rustic camp at the Black Bear Pool as well, which gives anglers the option of overnighting so they can fish the pool at first light. Each of the sections offers a different experience, and visitors rotate through."

Fishing the upstream stretches of the Hawke or Northwest Feeder, it will not be difficult to imagine yourself stepping off the pontoons of Lee Wulff's floatplane, being one of the lucky few to swing a fly across one of Labrador's wild salmon streams.

MIKE CROSBY was born and raised in Halifax, Nova Scotia. He has owned and operated a number of successful businesses over the past twenty-five years—including a sporting goods franchise, co-ownership of two salmon lodges, and Mike's Tackle Shop, a specialty fishing store that combines his business expertise with his passion for Atlantic salmon fishing. Mike has fished the salmon streams of eastern Canada for more than thirty-five years. He's even had the opportunity to "wet a line" with celebrities such as Robert Duval, Timothy Dalton, and Dennis Leary. Mike currently lives in Halifax with his wife, Ann, and their children, Mark and Heather. He is the author of *River Talk* (www.mikecrosby .com), which chronicles his lifelong love of salmon angling.

If You Go

▶ **Prime Time:** The brief season runs from late June through July.

▶ **Getting There:** The Hawke River is reached by floatplane from Charlottetown, Labrador. Guests reach Charlottetown via Goose Bay, Labrador, or Cornerbrook, Newfoundland, both of which are served by Air Canada (888-247-2262; www.aircanada .com). From either venue, you'll need to rent a car and drive to Charlottetown.

▶ **Accommodation/Guides:** Hawke River Outfitters (902-497-5444; www.hawkeriver outfitters.com) operates the only lodge on the Hawke River and provides guides as well as floatplane transportation from Charlottetown.

▶ **Equipment:** Mike Crosby recommends an 8-weight rod outfitted with floating line and 200 yards of backing. The lodge has a selection of proven patterns.

CAPE LOOKOUT

RECOMMENDED BY **Jake Jordan**

"I came home to Florida from a trip to Alaska back in 2002, and Chuck Furimsky asked if I could present at the Fly Fishing Show in Charlotte, North Carolina," Jake Jordan recalled. "I attended the show and was casting at one of the exhibition ponds with Steve Rajeff. A woman came up and said, 'You have the prettiest backcast I've ever seen. Do you mind if I cast that rod?' She stripped off more line than I had out, and made casts of 90 feet. She then introduced herself as Sarah Gardner, and said, 'My husband [Brian Horsley] and I fish for false albacore out of Harkers Island, near Cape Lookout.' I attended their seminar, and it was awesome. I asked when the fish were in, and she said in October and November. I told her that if she ever had an opening, I'd book a week, as I love catching powerful fish on a fly rod.

"A few weeks later, I got a call: 'We have a cancellation and can give you five or six days in November.' I booked, and took along one of my tarpon clients who lived in West Virginia. We got fish up to 18 or 19 pounds, and it was nothing for each of us to catch twenty or thirty fish in a day, sometimes on top water flies when the fish were on a bait ball. These fish are incredibly powerful and fast—faster in their initial 100-yard run than a bonefish of equal size and much stronger."

Cape Lookout rests at the bottom of the barrier islands off the mainland of North Carolina, south of the Outer Banks and Cape Hatteras National Seashore and east of Pamlico Sound. The sound is a rich nursery for many kinds of bait—glass minnows, sardines, crabs, and shrimp. (Pamlico Sound, incidentally, is the number two shrimp producer in the country.) Game fish take notice. And since Cape Lookout rests where the Labrador Current and Gulf Stream converge, there's a mix of game fish from northern and southern climes. "I lived and fished in the Keys for forty-six years, but I have to say

OPPOSITE:
Birds signal bait
balls, which off
Cape Lookout
in the fall signals
schools of big
false albacore.

DESTINATION

32

that the Cape Lookout region may be the best all-around saltwater fly fishing in the continental United States," Jake continued. "It's so good, I came here to retire. The albies were the first attraction. After I moved here, I began getting e-mails from people who told me about other aspects of the fishery—kingfish, Spanish mackerel, bluefish, modest-size redfish, the sea trout in the creeks, and the vast schools of gigantic redfish that show up in the fall. I remember being out albie fishing one October a few years back, and seeing what I thought was a large school of porpoises. I got closer, and the porpoises were orange . . . in fact, they were a school of 30- to 60-pound redfish, feeding on silversides! The school stretched 20 to 30 acres, about a quarter mile off the beach. I had seen such spawning schools in the Gulf before, but nothing like this!"

False albacore—known to marine biologists as little tunny—range throughout the temperate regions of the Atlantic, from New England to Old England, and South Africa to Brazil. They can reach weights of more than 30 pounds, though fish between 10 and 20 pounds are most common. They're frequently found close to shore and generally feed in the upper reaches of the water column, two things that endear them to anglers. As their popular name implies, they are frequently confused with other species designed for speed, including albacore, Atlantic bonito, and skipjack tuna. The little tunny is distinguished by its markings—dark spots behind its pectoral fins and wavy lines in its back—though anglers may more easily recognize albies by their pull. The fish usually arrive in the waters off North Carolina in late September, as Jake explained. "The shoreline areas of Pamlico Sound are fairly shallow, and when the first cold fronts come through, that shallow water cools pretty quickly. The deeper water takes longer to get cold, and the bait pushes out beyond the barrier islands when they feel the shock of the temperature drop. The game fish—including the albies—are waiting by the tens of thousands. We usually fish them by looking for bait balls. Once you find a bait ball [often indicated by the presence of birds], you kill the engine and cast in. There are times when you need to strip fast, other times when you need to let the fly sink down below the bait ball before you retrieve. I think size is more important than color when it comes to flies. I like smaller patterns with big eyes, generally on #6 or #8 hooks."

Anglers are not guaranteed encounters with football field–size schools of albies, though given a few days of fishing in October or November, your odds are very, very good. "I was out fishing with a friend, Buddy Rogers, near a spot called the Hook," Jake recalled. "The fog was very thick, but the water was dead calm. At one point, we saw three pelicans in the gloom. I let the boat drift to the pelicans. When they took off, the albies started in on the bait that had attracted the birds. From 8:00 until 12:00, we caught close to forty fish without ever turning the boat on. Buddy and I giggled like little kids. These fish were 8 to 20 pounds. I'd help Buddy land a fish, take the hook out, his fly would fall into the water, and a fish would hammer it. By noon, the fog started to clear, and we could suddenly see six other boats, all fishing their own bait balls."

With its reputation for long casts and heavy flies, the salt may not prove an ideal venue for tyros . . . though a fall day on Pamlico may change that perspective. "I had done a presentation—12 Months of Fly Fishing in North Carolina—at a fly-fishing club in Ocean City, New Jersey," Jake said. "A few days later I got a call from an attendee who wanted to book a few dates in October. When we hit the water that morning, I asked which hand he used to wind the reel. He said he wasn't sure. I asked him to show me his cast and he said, 'I'm not very good.' He waved the rod like a magic wand, and couldn't get the fly out of the boat. It turned out that the night at the club was his first contact with fly fishing. We took a few hours to teach him to cast. Pretty soon he was throwing 60 feet of line. In the process of his instruction, he landed seven albies, 7 to 10 pounds. He was pretty excited.

"Around 11:00, we heard a report from Brian and Sarah that they were on some big fish. I motored in their direction. Some big shapes were showing up on my fish finder, and I asked him to cast the sinking line out and let it sink. I told him to start stripping and suddenly a fish was on and off on a 200-yard run. 'I can't stop it,' he said, so I started the boat and we followed. Thirty minutes later, I got the leader in hand. It was a 24-pound false albacore, a world-record-class fish. He was exhausted, but I said, 'Come on, let's get another one.'

"Before the day was out, he'd caught a 45-pound redfish, four other big reds, and six more large albies. It was one of my best guiding days in North Carolina—he didn't know what had hit him."

CAPTAIN JAKE JORDAN has spent over half a century traveling the world in search of large game fish on the fly. He first gained acclaim as a Florida Keys tarpon guide; later he founded STH Reels and World Class Angler, an early Keys fly shop. Jake went on to launch the Bonefish School, a saltwater fly-fishing school held at the Peace & Plenty Bonefish Lodge in the Bahamas. He's a well-known speaker, author, and consultant to the boating and fly-fishing industries and has written for or been featured in most major sportfishing magazines. Jake is an FFF-certified fly casting instructor, an original member of the FFF advisory committee, and a charter member of the IGFA Certified Captains organization. Today, Jake guides anglers off the Keys during prime tarpon season, off the coast of North Carolina in the fall for albies and redfish, and operates the Sailfish School out of the Casa Vieja Lodge in Puerto San José, Guatemala, through the winter and Marlin Schools at locations around the world.

If You Go

▶ **Prime Time:** False albacore are present in strong numbers from early October through November.

▶ **Getting There:** The Coastal Carolina Regional Airport in New Bern is the closest commercial airport to Cape Lookout, and is served by US Airways (800-428-4322; www.usairways.com) and Delta Airlines (800-221-1212; www.delta.com). Raleigh/ Durham is 200 miles distant and served by most major carriers.

▶ **Accommodations:** Many anglers will use Morehead City as a base of operations. The Quality Inn (800-422-5404; www.moreheadhotels.com) comes well recommended.

▶ **Guides/Outfitters:** Several guides serve the waters of greater Pamlico Sound, including Jake Jordan's Fishing Adventures (252-444-3308; www.jakejordan.com); Brian Horsley and Sarah Gardner of Outer Banks Fly Fishing (252-449-0562; http://outer banksflyfishing.com); and Captain Joe Shute of Cape Lookout Fly Shop (800-868-0941; www.captjoes.com).

▶ **Equipment:** False albacore are powerful fish, and Jake recommends an 8- or 9-weight rod for fish below 10 pounds and a 10-weight stick for larger fish, with a spool of floating and intermediate line. On some occasions, a full-sinking line might come in handy. Surf Candy, Clousers, and Mushmouths will work; Jake likes the flies tied small, on #6 or #8 hooks.

DESTINATION

32

GREAT SMOKY MOUNTAINS

NATIONAL PARK

RECOMMENDED BY **Ian Rutter**

Great Smoky Mountains National Park straddles 800 square miles along the border of western North Carolina and southeastern Tennessee. Within a day's drive of nearly half of America's population, it's the nation's most popular national park, with upward of nine million visitors each year. Many come to see one of the park's 1,200 black bears, a symbol of wildness in the increasingly populous southeast. And more anglers are coming to lose themselves along the park's nearly 800 miles of trout streams in search of native southern Appalachian brook trout and wild rainbows and browns.

"I came to fishing through backpacking around the park," Ian Rutter began. "I'd see trout in the streams, and someone told me, 'If you want to catch trout, you have to fly fish.' So I learned to fly fish. While it seems that fly fishing has lost some of its popularity in the United States since it peaked after *A River Runs Through It*, we're seeing more anglers in the Smokies, as people can drive here for a weekend from Cincinnati or Atlanta and be back at work on Monday. Some prospective anglers say, 'Nine million visitors? No thanks!' But in truth, most people never leave their cars or the vicinity of their cars. If you walk ten or fifteen minutes up a trail, you're alone. If you walk an hour, you're in another time. It's exceedingly rare in the eastern United States to have such an expanse of wild country. The further up the streams you go, the more likely you are to find brook trout. These brookies are a distinct subspecies. The difference a casual viewer will notice is that the red shades on the fish are more vibrant. Biologists doing DNA tests are finding that these fish are further apart from northern brookies than rainbows and browns are."

Before the first rainbow trout from California's McCloud River were exported to the east and the first brown trout imported from Germany, brook trout were the only trout (well, technically char) east of the Mississippi. Even before the carpetbaggers arrived to displace them from much of their historic range, *Salvelinus fontinalis*—"the little salmon of the fountain"—were dwindling in numbers, thanks to stream degradation brought on by urban expansion and industrialization. The isolation of the Great Smokies' watersheds (and the region's subsequent national park status) helped protect many brookie populations from habitat destruction; though both browns and rainbows were successfully introduced in the thirties (and are now self-sustaining), the brookies have endured, often by retreating to the upper reaches of mountain streams. Hazel Creek, perhaps the best known of the Smokies' backcountry streams, is one brookie stronghold. "It's either a thirty-minute boat ride or a 20-mile hike to the mouth of Hazel Creek," Ian continued. "Once you're there, you're on foot. In the lower river there are browns and rainbows, but in the higher country, you'll find brook trout. Like anywhere in the park, these fish are not going to get larger than 10 inches, but they're beautiful to behold."

The fine trout waters in the Smokies are too plentiful to list here. Little River may be the best-known fishery, thanks in large part to its 15 miles of road access (you can continue on a trail for miles more). Deep Creek is the park's most noted brown trout stream. (Though fish are mostly below 12 inches in the park, browns can reach more than 20 inches on a few creeks.) "Many people assume that all the rivers are small here, but that's not the case," Ian said. "There are places you can go with a 6-foot weed whacker, but an 8- or 9-foot rod certainly fits in. Most of the watersheds have a pretty steep gradient, and most are extremely clear. There's a lot of pocket water high-sticking, whether the river's 15 or 60 feet wide. You can count on fishing mostly dry flies. If you follow a few rules, you'll do well: (1) Make sure you fish upstream. (2) Don't be in the water too much; if you do have to wade, don't go beyond your knees. (3) Wear drab colors. (4) Get a good drift.

"You can get fish that are much bigger outside of the park, but they are fish that are fed on agricultural products and they don't care if you wade right on them. The wild fish in the park take two or three years to grow. What you have to do to catch a 6-inch fish in Great Smoky National Park will prepare you to catch big fish elsewhere. If you have your A-game on from the Smokies, you'll knock 'em out in the Rockies.

"The fish in the park are exceptionally colorful. Add to that the brilliant wildflowers in the spring or the vibrant foliage of the fall, the crash of the water that envelops you as you cast into the next little pocket, the clear water that lets you watch the fish come to the fly. I can't imagine an angler that can't be happy fishing dry flies to beautiful native fish."

Iᴀɴ Rᴜᴛᴛᴇʀ has been fly fishing nonstop since the early 1990s. He scheduled his classes around fishing while at the University of Tennessee at Knoxville. Ian graduated with a bachelor of science in 1994 and began guiding fly fishers in 1995. He, with his wife, Charity, now operates R&R Fly Fishing from Townsend, Tennessee (just outside the park), guiding anglers on the streams of the Smoky Mountains and the tailwaters of eastern Tennessee and western North Carolina. Ian is on the pro staffs of Scott Fly Rods and Hyde Drift Boats. He's the author of *Great Smoky Mountains National Park Angler's Companion, Tennessee Trout Waters: Blue Ribbon Guide,* and *Rise Rings and Rhododendron: Fly Fishing the Mountain Streams and Tailwaters of Southern Appalachia.* Ian spends a good deal of time fly fishing in the Rocky Mountains every year and makes regular trips to saltwater destinations like Florida and Belize for bonefish, tarpon, permit, and redfish.

If You Go

▶ **Prime Time:** The Smokies are open year-round for fishing, but March through November provide the most reliable angling.

▶ **Getting There:** The western entrance of Great Smoky Mountains National Park (in Gatlinburg) is roughly 45 miles from Knoxville (served by most major carriers); the eastern entrance (in Cherokee) is 60 miles from Asheville (served by Delta Airlines and US Airways).

▶ **Accommodations:** The Great Smoky Mountains National Park website (www.nps.gov/grsm) includes links to town chambers of commerce near the park. R&R Fly Fishing (www.randrflyfishing.com) offers cabins just outside.

▶ **Guides/Outfitters:** Ian Rutter (866-766-5935; www.randrflyfishing.com) guides throughout the park, as does Steve Claxton (828-736-7501; www.steveclaxton.com) and Smoky Mountain Angler (865-436-8746; www.smokymountainangler.com).

▶ **Equipment:** A lighter rod in the 3- to 5-weight category with a floating line will work well in the Great Smoky Mountains. The outfitters above can help with flies.

DESTINATION

33

MÅLSELV RIVER

"Working around the fly-fishing travel world, I meet many international anglers who have checklists of the fisheries they must visit before they die," Mark Hewetson-Brown began. "The Målselv is not one of the Atlantic salmon rivers that appear on their radar—but for me, that's part of its appeal. It's not one of the big well-known rivers in Norway, but because of that it's relatively easy to access and is reasonably priced."

Next to New Brunswick, no area of the world may be more closely associated with Atlantic salmon—particularly *large* Atlantic salmon—than Norway. More than 600 rivers in this glacier-sculpted land support healthy fish runs. Tales of Norway's output are legend among salmon anglers—on one July evening in 1926, the Duke of Westminster landed thirty-three fish—a total of more than 800 pounds—including two beasts of 42 pounds and one of 45 pounds. (This epic outing transpired on the *grande dame* of Norwegian rivers, the Alta, which currently has a bit of a waiting list for beats . . . and a long line of interested parties eager to pay the tens of thousands of dollars the beats command.)

The Målselv rests above the Arctic Circle in Troms, Norway's second northern-most region. Non-angling visitors (and many Norwegians) may know the river for the Målselvfossen, a waterfall that is one of Norway's signature landmarks. Below the Målselvfossen, the Målselv seems devoid of the features that make a prime salmon stream; above the falls, it's another matter in a fishery marked by run after run of water begging to be swung through with a fly.

Like many fishermen's best finds, Mark came upon the Målselv by accident. "A fellow contacted me to see if I'd like to assess a fishing operation in northern Sweden," he recounted. "He said that he lived near a nice river in Norway, that we could do some fishing there too. I did an exploratory trip with two clients, and it was a disaster. The fellow

OPPOSITE:
The Målselv is lesser known than other Norwegian salmon rivers— and that's part of its appeal.

DESTINATION

34

was a charlatan. But one good thing did come out of it. He showed me the Målselv and introduced me to a guy named Tony Jacobsen. Tony is an ambulance driver, but more importantly, a hard-core angler. He fishes with his ambulance uniform under his waders and the ambulance by the riverbank. When the phone rings, he strips off his waders and heads off to wherever he's needed. Tony and I made arrangements to stay in touch, and I visited him the following year. I was struck with the river and the region, won over by the lack of development. The angling is very relaxed, fun, and old-fashioned. A case in point—I met a schoolteacher who camps by the river for the whole summer holidays. He can afford to rent the beat for the whole summer."

The Målselv may not kick out 40-plus-pound monsters with the consistency of the Alta to the north, but fish in the 20s are caught with some frequency, 30-plus-pound salmon show up each year, and 40-pound fish are rare but there. One of the pleasures of the fishery is the quality and diversity of its holding water. "There's not much in the way of big, slow pools," Mark said. "There are many classic runs with tailouts that are a joy to fish. It's not a beginner's river. To succeed, anglers have to be able to cast a fair line. If the river is up and dirty, you need to be able to throw a sinking line. The good news is the river clears extremely quickly. One day when I was out fishing, the river came up 3 feet in the morning. By the afternoon, it was clear."

Not surprisingly, a spey rod is the weapon of choice on the Målselv. Spey rods and spey casting have gained increasing traction in recent years among salmon and steelhead anglers who need to cover large pieces of water to locate their quarry. Instead of making a backcast—or multiple backcasts—to accelerate the fly line forward, spey casters use the tension of the water to harness the power of the longer spey rod (generally 12 to 16 feet in length) to make what resembles an exaggerated roll cast. With a modern spey rod in hand, casts of 80, 90, or 100 feet are well within the grasp of mere mortal anglers. The first spey rods were hewn from ash, and by all reports were not unlike wielding a tree branch. Even twenty-five years ago, two-handed rods were ungainly beasts. "When I was introduced to spey casting, the weapon of choice was the Double-Built Palakona manu-factured by Hardy," spey-casting expert Simon Gawesworth said. "It was 18 feet long, had two layers of split cane, and steel shaft in the middle. It weighed 54 ounces. It was a rod for *real* men." In the last few decades, many innovations in spey-casting technique and technology have come from Scandinavia, most notably from a Swedish angler named Göran Andersson. Andersson introduced an outfit that combined a shorter, stiffer spey rod with a shooting head and slick, small-diameter shooting line. Today this style is generally referenced as "Scandi-" or "Underhand-"style casting.

"Unlike some Norwegian rivers, fishing on the Målselv is all bank fishing," Mark added. "There are no boats paddling about in the middle of the river. The fish seem to like a slightly faster fly, so you cast a bit further down than you might on other rivers. The locals use chunky tippet material and really give the fish the beans once they're on. If you let the fish get into the fast water, they can make a mockery of you. Local riverkeepers are happy to see anglers from the UK or U.S.A., as nearly all of these visitors practice catch and release. When Norwegians catch a fish, it generally gets thumped, though many are trying to improve this."

During prime time on the Målselv the sun shines twenty-four hours—though fishing is limited to the period from 6:00 A.M. through midnight. "In the past, I've stayed at a guesthouse on the banks of the Målselv, a stone's throw from the beats we fish," Mark said. "I like to be on the river by six, come back for a late breakfast, head out again and have lunch on the river, then have dinner at the guesthouse and head back out for the evening's fishing. Many of the beats come with a simple cabin. If you want eighteen-hour access to your beat and are not bothered by camping, you can cook and warm up in the cabin (which has heat) and set up a tent outside for sleeping. During some of our after-dinner sessions, a friend of Tony's would join us at the cabin. He'd bring along smoked reindeer meat, which we'd fry up with some butter, wrap in bread, and wash down with some Aquavit—a true taste of Norwegian salmon fishing!"

MARK HEWETSON-BROWN is a long-standing member of the team at Frontiers Travel International, based in Gloucestershire, England. He joined Frontiers Ponoi River team in Russia in 2003, spending three seasons guiding at Ryabaga, while spending his winters working at the Frontiers U.S. office, coordinating driven shooting trips in Europe. Since October 2005 he has been a full-time member of Frontiers' European office, where he looks after shooting in Great Britain and Europe, shooting in South America, and fishing in Russia and South America. Mark spent the majority of his formative years with either a rod or gun in hand, either on the family farm in Hampshire or in southwest Ireland. He is a graduate of Newcastle University.

▶ **Prime Time:** The season on the Målselv runs from mid-June through September, with the middle portion of the season often providing the best fishing.

▶ **Getting There:** Guests generally fly into Tromsø, the primary air hub in northern Norway, which is served via Oslo. Several carriers provide service from the United States to Oslo, Norway, including SAS (800-221-2350; www.flysas.com) and Iceland Air (800-223-5500; www.icelandair.com). The village of Rundhaug is approximately two hours' drive from Tromsø.

▶ **Accommodations:** Many anglers fishing the Målselv will stay at Rundhaug Gjestegård (+47 77 83 05 70; www.rundhauggjestegard.no), a comfortable guesthouse near the river that also provides meals.

▶ **Guides/Outfitters:** Beats on the upper section of the Målselv are available from Frontiers Travel International (+44 845 299 6212; www.frontierstrvl.co.uk).

▶ **Equipment:** An 8-weight spey rod will enable a proficient caster to cover the water well on the Målselv. Reels should be outfitted with floating, intermediate sinking and sink-tip lines, with 200 yards of backing. Tube flies in black and blue work well.

METOLIUS RIVER

RECOMMENDED BY **John Judy**

If you were to venture over to central casting and request a trout stream, it's quite likely that the attendant would head into the warehouse and return with something closely resembling the Metolius River, a spring creek that can be as mystifying as it is beautiful.

"The Metolius has wonderful populations of native fish, both redband rainbows and bull trout," John Judy began. "They can be hard to locate, and for some that's frustrating. If you're impatient, you won't be rewarded. I find that it's very much a thinking man's river, as the Metolius always throws twists and curves at you. As much as I've researched it and tried to know it, it's still a mystery. But if you spend enough time out there, the river will occasionally lift up its veil and reveal itself. Just as quickly, the veil will drop back down."

For anglers and non-anglers alike, the beauty of the Metolius unfolds as you approach its headwaters near the settlement of Camp Sherman, 15 miles west of Sisters, in the heart of the Cascade Range of central Oregon. You can observe where its waters bubble up from the ground; its cold, clear flow is soon joined by several creeks, and within a few miles it's full-fledged river. As it flows 28 miles to Lake Billy Chinook (a reservoir created by the impoundment of the Metolius, Crooked, and Deschutes Rivers), it passes through thick stands of ponderosa pine and western red cedar, meadows of alpine wildflowers; a glance above the trees may offer a teasing glimpse of snow-capped Mount Jefferson. For anglers, the beauty of the surroundings extends to the river itself. The clear waters of the Metolius cascade in riffles and small falls over a basalt strata interspersed with ledges that drop off precipitously; you'll want to wade with caution. With perseverance, you'll get a close-up look at one of the river's handsome inhabitants—redband rainbows, resplendent in their bright pink and red stripes. Redband trout (*Oncorhynchus mykiss gairdneri*) are a

subspecies of rainbow trout native to the Fraser and Columbia River drainages east of the Cascade Mountains. Redbands, which can be distinguished by larger spots and white-tipped anal, dorsal, and pectoral fins, have the capacity to survive in warmer water than other rainbows . . . though that's certainly not an issue in the Metolius.

Unlike most western spring creeks, the Metolius has a healthy flow in addition to steady cold water temps. "There's about 35 feet of decline a mile, which makes the Metolius steeper and swifter than the average river," John continued. "It's also deep for a river its size. The pool-to-riffle ratio is low, and the fish are in very specific spots. Thanks to its spring origins, the river has very complex insect hatches. To complicate matters even more, the temperature changes as it goes downstream—it actually decreases—and this creates at least three or four microhabitats in the first 9 miles of the river alone (the section that's paralleled by an access road). A hatch that's occurring at mile three will probably not be happening at mile seven. Successful anglers will spend as much time looking as fishing. If you 'run and gun,' it won't be very effective, as some of the water that looks good doesn't hold fish. I like to look for deeper holes; these pools are major holding areas. In many of these pools, it may not be possible to get the fly to the bottom where the fish are, so you either need to wait for a hatch to bring them up or fish a shelf that drops into the deeper water. Once you find a good hatch that's occurring near decent holding water, the Metolius is no more complicated than any other river."

Though perhaps not as comely as the redbands, the bull trout of the Metolius pose a unique, and arguably more visceral, angling pursuit. Bull trout (*Salvelinus confluentus*) are indigenous to western North America, and require cold, clean water to thrive. (Some biologists will monitor bull trout populations to help gauge the overall well-being of a river system.) Technically a member of the char family, they are frequently confused with Dolly Varden, as they are quite similar in appearance. No one is sure of the origins of the name bull trout, though in *Trout and Salmon of North America*, biologist Robert J. Behnke conjectures that the name may apply to the stocky, flat head on larger fish or their aggressive feeding habits. Whatever the source of their moniker, no one will dispute the latter explanation; in fact, larger bull trout are predominantly piscivorous, or fish eating. In the Metolius, bulls can reach 30 inches and a weight of 15 pounds; they're sustained by whitefish, redbands, and kokanee salmon, which run up the river in the fall from Lake Billy Chinook to spawn. (Regulars on the Metolius will regale you with tales of whitefish or trout that have been snatched from their lines by opportunistic piscivores.)

OPPOSITE:
Deep holes and a steep gradient make the Metolius an especially challenging spring creek, and an especially beautiful one.

DESTINATION

35

The Metolius is open to catch-and-release bull trout fishing, one of the few such fisheries in the United States. The river's bull trout recovery project has served as a blueprint for other programs in the west.

"Bull trout are apex predators, and their bodies are built for capturing fish," John continued. "They'll respond to almost any streamer. I like to make things less complicated, as keeping flies off the bottom can be difficult. I like a simple conehead fly, not too heavy. White is the best color, as it connotes the color of sickness and injury. Fishermen can see it too. Rabbit fur gives the fly superb swimming action; it pushes water and simulates life. If I see a fish, I'll try to bounce it past on the bottom. Stack mending will help get the fly down, then it's puppet-on-a-string fishing—teasing the fly to make it flair up and settle. If you can make the fly look wounded, the bull trout will be stimulated and will come your way. I've had times when I've accidentally stuck the fly in the bottom. I'm not quick to pull it out, as sometimes fish will come over to inspect it. They'll watch it, I'll watch them, and we'll both wait. Sometimes it will take thirty seconds, but they'll eventually go and pick it out of the rocks."

What advice would John offer for first-time visitors to the Metolius: "Do your homework. Go to local fly shops; find out what's hatching. Then spend some time just looking up and down the banks. Spend as much time looking as fishing. Enjoy the scenery and control your expectations.

"Some days I go out there, the river doesn't give a lot. I take it for what it is. I go out the next day, shift my attack plan, and do well. When the veil lifts, that's when you really understand the Metolius and see its beauty."

JOHN JUDY is a well-known writer and fly-fishing guide, based in Camp Sherman, Oregon. He comes from a second-generation fly-fishing family and has been in the forefront of the development of many new and innovative fly-fishing techniques. His book *Slack Line Strategies* is considered by many to be the definitive primer on presentation skills. John's guide company, John Judy Fly Fishing (www.johnjudyflyfishing.com) is one of the oldest and best-established outfitters on the Deschutes River. The company fishes for both native trout and steelhead—specializing in presentation skills for trout and spey casting for steelhead. John has worked tirelessly to promote better fisheries management. He and a few friends successfully launched a campaign that resulted in the formation of Oregon Trout, Oregon's leading wild fish advocacy group. He also spent close to twenty years encouraging Fish and Wildlife to institute a very successful program on the Metolius River that ended stocking and brought back the native fish population (including the threatened and endangered bull trout). The quality of fishing on the Metolius and throughout Oregon has been greatly improved as a result of John's efforts. John is also the author of *Seasons of the Metolius* and a member of the Scott Fly Rod Pro Staff.

If You Go

▶ **Prime Time:** Much of the Metolius is open year-round, and there's always a hatch coming off. A favorite time for many anglers is June, when the green drake, a large mayfly, brings big redbands to the surface.

▶ **Getting There:** Camp Sherman is a three-hour drive from Portland, Oregon, which is served by most major carriers. Several carriers, including Alaska Airlines (800-252-7522; www.alaskaair.com) and United Airlines (800-864-8331; www.united.com), offer air service into Redmond, Oregon, which is roughly forty minutes from the Metolius.

▶ **Accommodations:** Pleasant cabins at or near the river are available from several properties, including Lake Creek Lodge (800-797-6331; www.lakecreeklodge.com) and Metolius River Lodges (800-595-6290; www.metoliusriverlodges.com). Many campsites are also available.

▶ **Guides/Outfitters:** Commercial guiding is not permitted on the Metolius, though several fly shops can help you navigate the complexities of its hatches, including The Fly Fisher's Place (541-549-3474, www.flyfishersplace.com) in Sisters and the Camp Sherman Store (541-595-6711; www.shermanstore.com).

▶ **Equipment:** A 5-weight rod outfitted with floating line will be fine for all redband angling, though when fishing drys, you could certainly go to a lighter rod. For hucking big streamers, most anglers prefer a 7- or 8-weight; John prefers a floating line to avoid hooking bottom. Check in at the fly shops above to get a sense of what flies might best suit river conditions.

DESTINATION

35

JOHN DAY RIVER

RECOMMENDED BY **Marty Sheppard**

Visit any Fish and Game Department branch office, and you're sure to see a "Take a Kid Fishing" poster. Beyond the mildly self-serving aspects of the promotion ("Keep Us Employed for Another Generation"), the Fish and Game folks have a point: Fishing brings families together in a peaceful place where modern-day distractions (like the latest online game) are largely out of reach, and there's the opportunity to simply talk . . . and perhaps even gain a better understanding of the natural world.

If the poster were to read "Take a Kid Fly Fishing," the smiling child in the photo might be gently releasing a smallmouth bass against a backdrop of the steep basalt canyons of central Oregon's John Day River. "Floating and fishing on the John Day for smallmouths are an extremely family-friendly experience," Marty Sheppard began. "The weather is dependably sunny and warm, the water temperature is perfect for swimming, the campsites are gorgeous, and there are plenty of fish. Kids can have just as much success as their skilled moms and dads . . . and just as much fun."

Running more than 500 miles between its three branches, the John Day is the third longest free-flowing stream in the United States; it's protected as a "wild and scenic river" under Oregon's Scenic Waterways Act. Home to the largest run of wild steelhead in the Lower 48, the John Day River is an unlikely smallmouth sanctuary. Bass are not endemic to Oregon, but back in 1971, seventy-five bass were surreptitiously introduced to the river. It would be an understatement to say that fish have prospered. Today, the John Day is considered one of the best bronzeback fisheries in the west. Large numbers of fish make for good catching—even beginning anglers can realistically expect to land up to fifty bass in a day. One-hundred-fish days are not uncommon for seasoned anglers happy with the smaller (10- to 12-inch) fish that rise readily—throughout the day—to popping bugs

OPPOSITE:
Tremendous
canyon scenery
and fast action
define a small-
mouth bass
float trip on
the John Day.

DESTINATION

36

slapped against the banks. "I have a lot of dads call and book trips," Marty continued, "and they say, 'I've got a six-year-old coming, I'm going to bring a spinning rod for him.' I tell them that they can certainly bring a spinning rod, but that we can have their little boy or girl fly fishing by the end of three days. At first, I'll try to put them right on top of the fish so they can dabble the fly over the fish—they'll take it. After a few hours of this, the kids will have a sense of where the fish are—in the foam lines and against the grass banks. They learn almost naturally. By day three, the six-year-old is casting 30 feet—and he's almost certain to be rewarded if he puts the fly where he should."

Marty has a bit of advice for adults trying to educate their kids about fly fishing: Lighten up. "I had a grandpa and grandson in the raft on one trip," he recalled, "and the grandpa was constantly on his grandson—'Ten o'clock, two o'clock, ten o'clock. Stop your rod!' The boy wasn't having any fun, and the grandpa was getting increasingly frustrated. That night I took the grandpa aside and said, 'I can make him a good caster, but you have to stop hounding him.' On the next day the grandpa backed off and the boy struggled a bit. But the third day, he was casting as far as his grandpa!"

The smaller bass that take top water flies provide constant and viscerally pleasing surface action, but they're not the only game in town. Deeper in the water column, bigger smallmouth await anglers seeking a greater challenge. "You don't get many larger bass on the surface on the John Day because the smaller bass beat them to the fly," Marty continued. "If you step up hook size a bit and can avoid hooking the small bass, you have a shot at bigger fish. Sometimes that means fishing deeper pools, other times it means targeting prime holding water in eddies. Bigger fish are slower-moving, methodical, ambush-style predators. They sit in the best lies waiting for crawdads, mayflies, and damselflies to drift by. From a presentation standpoint, you have to slow things down—a few strips, let the fly sit, a little twitch, let it sit. There are bass up to 24 inches in the John Day, but they're not easy. While we see a lot of families on the John Day, we also see quite a few guys who make the fly-fishing travel rounds—anglers who fish chinooks in Alaska, tarpon in the Caribbean, roosterfish in Baja. I think what brings them back is that it's a fishery where you can find several different kinds of success. You can spend some time catching many smaller fish, then step up the challenge and focus on the big ones."

The isolated canyons of the John Day—sometimes called the Grand Canyon of Oregon—provide a majestic backdrop for a bassing adventure. (While some small sections of the river are open to anglers on foot, most prefer to raft the river, generally for three to six days.) Floating past imposing rock formations of vertical basalt and abandoned cabins of early homesteaders, you may spot bighorn sheep, pronghorn antelope, or mule deer on the cliffs, and golden eagles, bald eagles, and pygmy owls on the wing. "Many sections of the canyon have a haunted feeling," Marty added. "You half expect a band of Indians to become visible over the canyon rim. Several Native American tribes once called the valleys home, including the Northern Paiute. In the course of a float, we'll stop at several places to show remnants of Indian life—pit house foundations with obsidian shrapnel scattered about, petroglyphs [incised rock art], and pictographs [drawn rock art]. It's a spiritual moment in the course of our float."

When the nip of fall can be felt in the air and the waters cool, the smallmouth become less active . . . and the steelhead return. In October, before the cold takes hold, fish can be quite willing to take skated flies. "It's an amazing steelhead river, a testament to how well these wild fish populations can do when they're just left alone. On many rivers, all the steelhead you catch look about the same. On the John Day, every fish looks different."

MARTY SHEPPARD grew up on the banks of the Sandy River in Oregon and landed his first steelhead at the age of five. Today, he guides year-round (with his wife, Mia) on the John Day, Sandy, Grande Ronde, and Klickitat Rivers. Marty is a supporter of the Native Fish Society and serves on the board of WaterWatch of Oregon.

If You Go

► **Prime Time:** The John Day fishes best from early June through mid-August.

► **Getting There:** Most visitors fly into Portland, which is served by many major carriers. From there, it's a two-and-a-half-hour drive to Condon, where trips stage.

► **Accommodations:** On the river you'll stay in comfortable tents and enjoy camp meals. Condon, where you'll stay before the trip launches, has two lodging options: Condon Motel (541-384-2181) or the Hotel Condon (800-201-6706; www.hotelcondon.com).

► **Guides/Outfitters:** Little Creek Outfitters (503-944-9165; www.littlecreekoutfitters .net) specializes in fly-fishing floats on the John Day.

► **Equipment:** A 4- or 5-weight outfitted with floating line is ideal; a 6- or 7-weight with floating line and a few sink tips will work well if you go after bigger bass.

DESTINATION

36

OUTER ATOLLS

RECOMMENDED BY **Henry Gilbey**

"If fly fishing was originally designed as the gentle art," Henry Gilbey declared, "then hunting giant trevally takes the sport to a whole different level. GTs are a seriously bad fish that should be seeking help for an immense aggression problem. The flats around the Outer Atolls of the Seychelles are crawling with sharks and there are deadly cone shells underfoot, but if I were to be an animal out there, I'd choose to be a GT. They rule."

The Seychelles are an archipelago of 115 islands scattered over 150,000 square miles in the Indian Ocean, roughly 1,000 miles off the coast of Kenya, and 600 miles north of Madagascar . . . which is to say, not particularly close to anywhere! From their discovery in 1502, the Seychelles bounced back and forth between French and English control before gaining independence in 1976. Historically, the islands' inhabitants relied on cotton cultivation, whaling, coconut plantations, and the export of guano for economic sustenance. Since gaining independence, the government has set aside nearly half of the country's total area as nature reserve or parks, and tourism has flourished. (In the last decade, this has become the tropical getaway of choice for celebrities like Paul McCartney and Pierce Brosnan.) Far from any mainland and riding the equator, the Seychelles present as idyllic a tropical environment as one might imagine. The air temperature hovers around 85 degrees year-round; the water temperature is the same. The water is incredibly clear, and its turquoise tones are offset by the white, white sand and swaying palm trees.

Sportfishing-oriented tourism came to the Seychelles in the late nineties, with operations based around Alphonse Island, roughly 150 miles south of Mahe, the island nation's capital. Thanks in part to a South African outfitter called FlyCastaway, the frontier of Seychelles fly fishing has pushed even farther off the grid, to a region broadly described as the Outer Atolls. Between 400 and 600 nautical miles south of Mahe, these include

OPPOSITE:
An angler brings a giant trevally to hand off the Outer Atolls of the Seychelles.

DESTINATION

37

Cosmoledo, Assumption, Astove, Farquhar, and Providence. (Cosmoledo, Assumption, and Astove are part of the Adalbra Group, home of the Adalbra tortoise, which reaches a weight of more than 500 pounds and can live upward of 150 years.) Farquhar Atoll is home to a small lodge; expeditions to the other atolls unfold aboard a live-aboard "mother ship" that's outfitted with several tender boats to bring anglers into the flats. "You feel very insignificant on a flat in the Outer Atolls," Henry added. "These islands represent one of the most remote saltwater-angling destinations in the world." Once there, you can expect regular encounters with big bonefish, milkfish (an algae feeder that's been described as leaping like a tarpon and tearing line off a 9-weight twice as fast as a big bonefish), a host of triggerfish species, Indo-Pacific permit . . . and, of course the GT. (Some fly-fishing travel purveyors have referred to Cosmoledo and Providence Atolls as the world's GT headquarters!)

The largest of the thirty species of trevally, giant trevally (*Caranx ignobilis*) are indigenous to the Pacific and Indian oceans. Around the Outer Atolls of the Seychelles, GTs run from 20 to 120 pounds and terrorize the flats when tides permit, preying on bonefish and about anything else they can catch. Though they move quickly, their size and swagger make them unmistakable when they move up onto the flats to ambush some unfortunate creature. Henry vividly recalls his first GT encounter at Cosmoledo. "My guide called out, 'Geet, geet, moving fast, three o'clock, cast, cast, put that fly down hard.' I saw a big, black shape that was beyond a doubt a GT. With fumbling, shaking hands, I managed an attempt at a cast. The fly slapped down hard nowhere near the vicinity of the fish. The guide implored me to 'strip, strip, fast, keep going!' I could see that black shape turn and literally charge my fly down so hard that it was all I could do to stop myself freezing to the spot in complete terror. After all, we were meant to be going after the fish, not the other way around! Like a fool, I lifted the fly right out of the way in some daft attempt at a strike. This didn't put the fish off. In fact, it seemed to drive the fish even madder. 'Where's the fly!' the fish seemed to be implying as it surged madly around us. 'Put the fly down hard, right there, go, go, strike now!' the guide begged. I strip-striked and wanted to beam a smile at my guide as I knew I'd hooked up . . . but suddenly I had a rampaging beast on the end of my line, intent on taking it all. Brutal, savage, unrelenting—these are the words I would use to describe a contest with a GT. Some fish, you *play*; GTs, you *fight*."

Numbers at Cosmoledo can be off-the-charts impressive: on several occasions, a group of eight anglers landed more than 400 GTs in the course of a week. But it takes some work. "It's hot as hell and very humid," Henry added. "The longer you can walk, the more fish you can find. I had one afternoon when the tides were strong, and there were large GTs—including one fish over one hundred pounds—corralling bait on a flat we were wading. The fish were so big and excited, I was quite uncomfortable." (GTs are not the only fearsome predator on the flats of Cosmoledo. In April 2009 the *Indian Ocean Explorer* was hijacked by Somali pirates. The crew was safely released, but for a time, fishing operations around Cosmoledo were curtailed. As of this writing, operations have renewed, with security personnel on board.)

If you can pull yourself away from the GTs or the pursuit of bonefish approaching the 10-pound mark, the Outer Atolls hold other treasures. The blue-water fly fishing can be sensational for sailfish, dogtooth and yellowfin tuna, and wahoo; the fish are close enough to the atolls that they can be hunted from the tenders. If you opt to stay on the flats, you can likely take a shot at creatures more often found in the depths by scuba divers—including psychedelically shaded bumphead parrotfish. "I was walking a flat on Providence Atoll, and could feel vibrations—it was the bumpheads feeding on coral. Sometimes, you'd see them tailing like bonefish, except their tails are the size of my head. The guys were fishing white Velcro crabs. Bumpheads have a sharp beak, and unless they were hooked in the right place, they'd break off right away. When one fish was hooked, the others would spook, and it would sound like a herd of hippos racing away. Generally they're not legitimate fly quarry as they tend to be deepwater fish. But at Providence (and some of the other atolls) they come on the flats regularly. They can be targeted, and they pull some proper string."

HENRY GILBEY has a serious problem—a lifelong addiction to fishing. Ten years ago, it was getting so bad that he had to explore a way of making fishing a livelihood. Today, he works as a writer, photographer, TV presenter, and consultant, focused on fishing. (In the spirit of full disclosure, Henry will occasionally use a spinning rod as well as a fly rod!) His television work includes *Fishing with Henry* (don't you just love that original title), *Fishing on the Edge*, *Wild Fishing*, and *Wild Fishing 2*. His photography and writing have appeared in many publications, including *Adventure Fishing*, the *London Times*, *Fishing Wild*, *Gray's Sporting Journal*, and *Sport Fishing*, and his angling adventures have taken him around the world, from Angola to Canada. Henry calls Cornwall, England, home. See samples of his work at www.henry-gilbey.com.

▶ **Prime Time:** The first part of the season traditionally runs from early November to mid-December and the second part from late February to mid-April, with a break over the festive season, as January is one of the rainiest months in the Seychelles.

▶ **Getting There:** Mahe, the principal island of the Seychelles, is served with flights from various European gateway cities via Air Seychelles (+248 381 000; www.airseychelles .net), British Airways (800-247-9297; www.britishairways.com), and Kenya Airways (866-536-9224; www.kenya-airways.com). From Mahe, a chartered aircraft will take you to Farquhar or Assumption Atoll, where you'll join the mother ship, which will be home for your journey. (There's also a lodge operation on Farquhar Atoll.)

▶ **Guides/Outfitters:** South Africa–based FlyCastaway (+27 82 334 3448; www.flycast away.com) specializes in adventure fly-fishing excursions to the Outer Atolls of the Seychelles.

▶ **Equipment:** For giant trevally, you'll need a stout 12-weight rod equipped with a floating line and at least 400 yards of backing. Proven patterns include the Clouser Minnow, Sea Habit, Merking Crab, and Sliding Head Popper, all in 6/0 or 8/0—not something you're likely to find at your local fly shop!

DESTINATION

37

SOČA RIVER

RECOMMENDED BY **Rok Lustrik**

Mainland Europe is not awash in trout streams—or at least not in trout streams that read-ily roll off the tongue. For years, Rok Lustrik has been single-handedly trying to introduce anglers to the possibilities of continental trouting. And as more fly anglers make their way to Slovenia, he will have many willing acolytes.

"Slovenia is a very small nation," Rok began. "It's only a three-hour drive from east to west, and a two-hour drive north to south. But within this small area, there are two major watersheds. One—the Sava—flows into the Danube, and ultimately drains to the Black Sea. This system has rainbow trout, brown trout, grayling, and a larger salmonid, the Danube salmon (or husen, a close relative of the taimen). The other watershed—the Soča—drains to the Adriatic, and is home to rainbow, gold-colored Adriatic grayling, and marble trout, a great game fish that's indigenous to the region. The rivers provide tre-mendous variety. There are freestone rivers like those you find in New Zealand, and chalk streams like the River Test. The rivers are very clean; most are very clear. On a weeklong fishing trip, you won't see the same kind of river twice."

Once annexed under the republic of Yugoslavia, Slovenia is a republic whose iden-tity—let alone location—may be little known to North Americans. The small mountain-ous nation is on the Balkan Peninsula, bordered by Austria to the north, Hungary to the northeast, Croatia to the south and southeast, and Italy and the Adriatic Sea to the west. Physically balanced between eastern and western Europe, Slovenia strikes a happy blend between the Italian, Austrian, and Slavic cultures that have come to bear upon it. "In my opinion, it is difficult to make generalizations about Slovenia," Rok continued. "In the north, it has an alpine flavor in terms of food and culture. In the south close to Italy, it more mirrors Mediterranean customs. Wherever you go, it's very safe, and the

171

café culture thrives; you'll always find people sitting outside on town squares, sipping coffee, wine, or beer. Another thing that's true for most of Slovenia is that we're on the drier side of the Alps, which run along our western border."

Of Slovenia's many rivers, the Soča may be its most famous. Beginning in the Trenta Valley in the Julian Alps, it flows in a southerly direction along the Italian border, entering the Adriatic near the Italian town of Monfalcone. Two things make the Soča stand out: first is its color, a distinctive emerald green, almost the shade of a glacial river, but clear. "People think the Soča's color is the result of snowmelt, but that's not the case," Rok explained. "It's due to ground limestone at the bottom of the river that reflects the light." The second special aspect of the Soča is its marble trout. "There are a few river systems in Croatia and Italy that have marble trout, but they're nearly extinct there," Rok said. "In Slovenia, the marble almost became extinct; now they're off the endangered list. The Soča and its tributaries have the largest population anywhere." Distinguished by the marble pattern on its skin, these fish can grow to 50 pounds or more. Marble trout behavior is somewhat akin to that of bull trout in North America; younger fish will feed on insects, but as they grow larger, their diet centers on other fish.

"Marble trout are everywhere in the Soča, but they are challenging to catch," Rok continued. "It's mostly sight-fishing. We'll walk along a bit, spot a fish, and see how it's acting. If the fish is sitting on the bottom, odds are low that it will be interested in a fly. If it's out in the current feeding, you have a better chance."

A trip to Slovenia is as much a chance to revel in the charms of a little explored part of Europe as it is an opportunity to wet a line. To that end, Rok suggests a weeklong tour de force.

"If I had a week, I'd probably begin around the town of Bled, which is consistently ranked as one of alpine Europe's most picturesque villages. It just so happens that the Sava Bohinjka flows nearby. I'd spend some time on the Sava Bohinjka and the main stem of the Sava after the two tributaries come together. On a normal day, I'd expect you to catch twenty fish—mostly rainbows, with some brown trout and grayling mixed in. On summer evenings, there will be some nice hatches. We have many of the same insects North American anglers would be familiar with—Blue-Wing Olives, midges, even salmon flies. Generally, Sava fish will not rise to drys unless there's a hatch, so we nymph until bugs begin coming off. The second half of the week, I'd focus on the Soča and some of its tributaries.

OPPOSITE:
The Soča's distinctive shade and resident marble trout make it the jewel of Slovenian fly fishing.

DESTINATION

38

"A few years back, I had a guest named Jeremy who really wanted to catch a marble trout. I planned to take him to the Idrijca, as it had been raining and that river can fish well when it's a little high. The night before our outing, I had dream that Jeremy had a big marble trout take the fly trailing off his streamer, but I hadn't tied the trailer hook firmly on, and the fish came off. The next morning we got to the Idrijca and the water was high and a little off-color—good marble trout conditions. I told Jeremy of my dream and double-checked the knot on the trailer fly. Jeremy cast a streamer over a pool, and a marble followed the fly and seemed to grab. Jeremy set the hook, but there was nothing. He made a second cast, and the same thing happened. Then a third and a fourth cast. Still nothing. On the fifth cast, the fish took the fly hard. Soon, Jeremy landed a 17-pound marble trout."

ROK LUSTRIK has been an enthusiastic fly angler and fly tier for nearly twenty years. He is a professional guide and founder of Lustrik Fishing Adventures (www.lustrik.com). Rok feels truly privileged to have been born and to live in Slovenia, a country that can offer so wide a variety of fishing options, from gin-clear alpine streams to mysterious chalk streams.

If You Go

▶ **Prime Time:** The trout fishing season in Slovenia extends from March to November; July and August provide the best hatches (and weather). Anglers must purchase daily beat privileges for the river they hope to fish; prices range from €50 to €100.

▶ **Getting There:** Visitors to Slovenia generally fly into Ljubljana, which is served by Air France (800-237-2747; www.airfrance.com) and Lufthansa (800-399-5838; www.lufthansa.com).

▶ **Accommodations:** The Bled tourism website (www.bled.si/en) outlines lodging options in this picturesque town. Rok's website (www.lustrik.com) lists other options.

▶ **Guides/Outfitters:** There are several guide services in Slovenia, including Rok's company (www.lustrik.com) and Slovenia Flyfishing (+44 1257 464996; www.sloveniaflyfishing.com).

▶ **Equipment:** A 4- or 5-weight rod outfitted with floating line is good for the smaller streams; a 6-weight, fast-action rod is best for marble trout. Patterns used on North American streams will work here.

VAAL RIVER

RECOMMENDED BY **Gerhard Laubscher**

When outsiders think of Africa and freshwater fly fishing, it's generally tiger fish that spring to mind. In South Africa, fly anglers' thoughts drift instead to a species that has little notoriety outside of their country's borders—yellowfish. "Yellowfish are indigenous to South Africa, particularly the Vaal and Orange Rivers," Gerhard Laubscher explained, "but it's only in the past ten years or so that people have really become passionate about fishing for them. Twenty years ago if you wanted to fly fish in freshwater, you'd likely fish for trout. All trout in South Africa are introduced, and the fisheries—often still waters—are syndicated and very expensive. When you contrast fishing by a dam for stocked fish with wading a wide river, catching endemic species, it's hardly any comparison. Yellowfish will take a variety of insects, they fight very hard, and the rivers they swim in are convenient to Johannesburg and Pretoria. If the river is behaving the way it's supposed to, I can pretty much guarantee a visiting angler a fish of 6 pounds, and perhaps a total of thirty or forty fish to hand."

Yellowfish are members of the genus *Labeobarbus*, and are relatives of barbel, a carplike species found in some river systems in Europe and Asia. They're distinguished by the namesake color of their scales, which range from silver with a hint of yellow to a rich gold. There are nine species of yellowfish in South Africa, though anglers focus almost exclusively on two—smallmouth and largemouth. Smallmouth prefer faster flowing waters with a rocky or sandy substrate and are catholic feeders, consuming baitfish, crustaceans, and a variety of aquatic insects. Smallmouth yellowfish approaching 20 pounds have been landed, though fish average between 3 and 4 pounds.

The Vaal River is the epicenter of smallmouth yellowfishing in South Africa. It begins in the Drakensberg Mountains in the Mpumalanga province and flows nearly 700 miles

in a southwesterly direction until it joins the nation's largest river, the Orange, near Kimberley. Yellowfish are found the length of the river, though Gerhard focuses his efforts on the upper and middle sections of the river. "The Upper Vaal flows through the Highveld, a higher-altitude plains environment east of Johannesburg," he continued. "It's largely agricultural country. The Middle Vaal is southwest of Johannesburg, and flows through the Bushveld in the Northwest province. It's a bigger river here, and the flora and fauna are more diverse than on the Upper Vaal—perhaps closer to what a visitor's perception of Africa might be. Where the Upper Vaal is mostly smallmouth yellowfish, the Middle also has sections with good populations of largemouth. 'Vaal' is Afrikaans for pale, and anglers should not be put off by the river's murky, brown color. The fish will always take flies."

If fish aren't actively rising, Gerhard will usually begin prospecting with nymphs. "We fish upstream, with two flies in tandem, and a strike indicator above," he described. "You try to achieve a dead drift. We use fairly sturdy tippet—3x or 4x—as the fish know how to use the current, and when you get a 4- or 5-pound fish on, you've got to have your act together to maintain control." Closer to the headwaters of the Vaal catchment, a more delicate experience awaits. "There's a lake called Sterkfontein that has no streams or agricultural runoff flowing into it, and no muddy areas on its banks, so it stays very clear," Gerhard continued. "There are great amounts of terrestrial insects around the lake, and the fish focus on beetles and grasshoppers when the wind is blowing. When conditions are right, you'll have nonstop dry-fly activity. You'll have some fish that will come up and inspect a fly three or four times—even bump it with their nose—and then drop back down and not eat it. Here, you need 6x or 7x. When you hook one of these fish, you can't try to stop it. You just have to let it go and hope the tippet holds. The colors here are fantastic—green mountains, blue water, and golden fish."

During the early summer, the Highveld is susceptible to violent thunderstorms. Once the storms have passed, the Upper Vaal can see some of its most prolific hatches. Gerhard still recalls one such an epic occurrence—one that he was unable to fully appreciate. "I had a client who was a very new angler, and I took him up to one of my favorite sections of the river. The clouds were still lingering from the storm the previous day, but the river was crystal clear. On the pool below me, there were rising fish as far as I could see. Fishing the pool would probably be the best dry-fly opportunity either of us would ever have. But I didn't think he'd be able to make the casts he'd need to make. I must have

OPPOSITE:
The Vaal does not always flow clear, but its yellowfish are ever eager to take a well-presented fly, even in murky water.

DESTINATION

39

debated what to do for ten minutes before I took him upstream to a set of rapids, as it would be easier fishing. I think he hooked nine or ten fish before I was able to show him how to set the hook and land one. Meanwhile, every time I looked back at the pool, the fish were rising. It was killing me.

"After he landed a few more, I told him 'Bear with me, I'm going to show you something special.' I brought him down to the pool and we stood on a rock. He caught three or four fish on a dry fly while I looked on. I don't know if he understood how special this hatch was. I've never seen rising fish like that again."

GERHARD LAUBSCHER is one of the founders of FlyCastaway, which leads fly anglers on adventures throughout Africa, the Indian Ocean islands, and other unexplored regions of the world. His saltwater fishing and guiding have taken him to all the outer atolls of the Seychelles, St. Brandon's, Madagascar, and the entire coastline of Mozambique, Kenya, Angola, and Gabon. His focus on southern Africa's indigenous freshwater species like tiger fish and yellowfish has made him a forerunner in these fields. Gerhard has designed numerous freshwater and saltwater fly patterns that are used all over the world today and has been especially influential in the development of the patterns and techniques used for largemouth yellowfish.

If You Go

▶ **Prime Time:** The Vaal fishes consistently from September to April.

▶ **Getting There:** Johannesburg is near to the Vaal, and is served by many carriers.

▶ **Accommodations:** Some will opt to stay in Johannesburg, and accommodations here are highlighted at the city's website (www.joburg.org.za). The town of Parys is on the banks of the Vaal; lodging options here are highlighted at www.parys.co.za.

▶ **Guides/Outfitters:** Several guides, including FlyCastaway (+27 82 334 3448; www.fly-castaway.com) and Mavungana (+27 13 254 0270; www.flyfishing.co.za), fish the Vaal.

▶ **Equipment:** A 5- to 7-weight rod outfitted with floating line will suffice for yellowfish. Many common trout patterns will work for yellowfish.

DESTINATION 39

PORT O'CONNOR

RECOMMENDED BY **Kevin Townshend**

In 2002, Kevin "KT" Townshend missed his annual pilgrimage to Homosassa in search of giant tarpon. He would soon learn that it wasn't necessary to leave Texas to find silver kings.

"I grew up in north Texas, and even though my grandfather was a freshwater fishing and hunting guide and we traveled around in the field, I never spent any time on the Gulf Coast," KT recalled. "It was seven hours away, like a different state. Though I'd visited the Bahamas and Belize, I didn't make my first saltwater fly-fishing trip in Texas until I was thirty-five. I fell in love with the redfishing. I was amazed at what an incredibly large coastline Texas has, how diverse it is from north to south, and how pristine, despite being close to some sizable cities. After my missed trip, I was singing the blues at a fly shop in Tyler, Texas. The owner said I should lighten up and go see a guide named Scott Graham over in Port O'Connor, that he was sight-fishing to big tarpon. I said, 'Come on, you can't sight-fish for big tarpon in Texas!' But he insisted you could, so I made a date to go fishing with Scott. We went out, and I made two casts. On the first, I hooked and landed a 140-pound fish. On the second, I hooked and landed a 160-pound tarpon.

"That was enough to convince me to move back to Texas from the Rocky Mountains, where I'd been for seventeen years. I fell in love with Port O'Connor through a love for tarpon."

Port O'Connor is a sleepy town near the center of the 790-mile-long Texas coast, midway between Galveston and Corpus Christi. Several geographic characteristics combine to make it a saltwater angler's haven, as KT explained. "First, you have immediate access to blue water for pelagic species like mackerel and tuna. You can run as little as 2 miles and find these fish. Second, there are two big bays north and south of Port O'Connor—

DESTINATION

40

Espiritu Santo and Matagorda. Both bays have excellent redfish habitat, and in just about any weather conditions you can find some protected shoreline to fish. Most importantly, Port O'Connor is situated right across from the Pass Cavallo. This is the only natural entrance to the bay system until you reach Port Aransas. The tarpon have this pass deeply imprinted in their migration memory. The feeding possibilities the pass provides, combined with the deep pockets of water present in each bay—deep enough for fish to find cover—makes Port O'Connor a place where migratory tarpon want to stop and spend some time."

Historically, mature tarpon have been frequent visitors to the Gulf waters of the Texas coast. At one time, the runs were so great that Port Aransas was called Tarpon. In the sixties, however, the fish abruptly disappeared from Texas waters. "There are many theories of why this happened, and why the fish have made a reasonably good comeback," KT ventured. "I believe there are three main reasons they've rebounded: one, that the fish are not being killed as frequently in Mexico, thanks to stricter regulations that resulted from the realization that live fish are worth more from a tourism perspective; two, that several Mexican refineries that were dumping pollutants into the Gulf have cleaned up their act considerably; and three, there's been a reduction in the amount of fertilizers and insecticides funneling into the Gulf from Texas rivers." Several studies are currently under way in an effort to better understand the habits of tarpon that migrate along the Gulf Coast, in hopes of furthering future conservation efforts. These include a satellite tagging and tracking program spearheaded by Tarpon Tomorrow, and the Tarpon Genetic Recapture Program (created by the Florida Fish and Wildlife Conservation Commission's Fish and Wildlife Research Institute), which educates anglers on how to save DNA "fingerprints" from caught fish to track their movements. "I love catching tarpon and guiding anglers to them," KT added, "but I'm also an avid tarpon observer. I jumped at the chance to get involved with these programs. The more I get to know about these fish, the more I realize that I don't know very much at all about them."

Most fly anglers visiting Port O'Connor hope to find a tarpon—preferably leaping at eye-level on the end of their shock tippet 20 or 30 feet away. But they're also curious to get a taste of the redfishing. An average summer or early fall day in Port O'Connor involves both. "There are three other guides chasing tarpon out of Port O'Connor," KT said, "and we start the day by figuring out where each guy is going to fish. I used to work on the Green River in Utah, where you can have ninety guides working, and learned that working together makes for a better experience for everyone. I like to start in one of the bays. You can tell pretty quickly by the water clarity and how much bait is splashing if it's going to be happening or not. When people think of tarpon fishing in Texas—*if* they think of it—they picture rolling fish. When conditions are right, I have sandbars around Port O'Connor in crystal clear water that are like those you find off the Florida panhandle. You can pick up cruising fish 300 or 400 feet away. If we don't find fish in the bay, we'll head out to Pass Cavallo. If we don't find any tarpon there, we have a choice: we can either motor back into the bay or to Matagorda Island to hunt redfish, or head out to the jetties and continue tarpon fishing. Casting into the rocks is my least favorite way of catching them, but the fish are there, and any tarpon in the air is a good tarpon!"

One of the unwritten rules of guiding is "Never catch your client's fish." This rule is underscored when the quarry is a hard-to-find fish like a steelhead or a tarpon. Much to his chagrin, KT had a week in the summer of 2010 where he broke the rule three times! "We were fishing out at the jetties, and my client was having a tough time casting a sink tip. He wanted to switch to an intermediate line. I told him that the intermediate would not get the fly to where the fish were, but he couldn't believe that it mattered. When he took a break casting the intermediate, I made one cast with the sink tip and hooked a 60-pound fish. 'How did that happen?' he cried. 'The sink tip gets 2 feet closer to the fish,' I said. Two days later, it was the same situation. A fellow was struggling with the sink tip and finally said, 'Show me how to do it.' He'd made eighty casts with nothing. On my second cast, I hooked a 150-pounder. I felt terrible. He kept fishing, but was dejected, having hell with the sink tip. Finally, he said, 'I'll try the intermediate.' I handed him the other rod and sat on the poling platform, with the rod over my shoulder. The fly was dangling 2 inches under the surface. As he's stripping line out to cast, my shoulder almost gets ripped off. A tarpon had grabbed it and was up in the air behind us. He looked at me with exasperation, and I pleaded, 'I swear, I didn't cast!'"

KEVIN TOWNSHEND is a fly fisherman and upland bird hunter who seeks outdoor adventure wherever it leads. Many are chronicled on *KT Diaries* (www.ktdiaries.com), a television series that's widely distributed throughout Texas, Louisiana, and Arkansas. KT guided for nearly two decades on Utah's Green River, but now calls Port O'Connor home—though during the winter he guides for pheasants in Nebraska. His fly-fishing travels have taken him throughout the American West, the Caribbean, and, of course, Texas.

▶ **Prime Time:** Migratory tarpon are present around Port O'Connor from June through October, with late summer being peak season.

▶ **Getting There:** The nearest commercial airport to Port O'Connor is in Corpus Christi, which is served by several carriers, including American Airlines (800-433-7300; www.aa.com) and Continental Airlines (800-523-3273; www.continental.com).

▶ **Accommodations:** There are several lodging options in Port O'Connor, including 10th Street Lodge (361-983-2281; www.10thstreetlodge.com) and the Poco Loco Lodge (361-983-0300; www.thepocolocolodge.com).

▶ **Guides/Outfitters:** Several guides hunt tarpon around Port O'Connor, including Kevin Townshend (307-389-2732; www.ktdiaries.com) and Scott Graham (828-682-0128; www.flyfishingtexas.com).

▶ **Equipment:** A 12-weight with a sturdy reel and spools of intermediate and sink-tip fly lines, plus at least 300 yards of backing, will prepare you for Texas tarpon. Guides have rods available, and supply popular flies.

DESTINATION 40

LLANO RIVER

RECOMMENDED BY **Tim Romano**

"When a lot of people think of freshwater and Texas, they think of farm ponds and muddy creeks," Tim Romano began. "That's not the case in the Hill Country. The rivers there are some of the most beautiful I've ever seen. Most are spring fed by the Edwards Aquifer. Some are gin clear, even at depths of 20 feet. Others have a remarkable aquamarine tint. Some have white limestone bottoms, others granite. Coming from Colorado, I thought I knew clear water, but these rivers have incredible visibility. I could take nine out of ten fly fishermen out on these exotically scenic rivers, and they wouldn't believe they're in Texas."

The Hill Country can be roughly defined as the region stretching 100 miles west from the cities of Austin (in the north) and San Antonio (in the south)—though Tim pointed out that some Texans might beg to differ on where the region begins and ends. One thing is for sure—the ocean that once covered the region receded and the seafloor rose eons ago, and the limestone hills that define this region of central Texas and the aquifer that provides the lifeblood for its waterways began to take shape. There are a number of rivers that anglers can explore here. The Llano, San Marcos, and Devils Rivers are a few of the attractions for fly fishers. Each has its own character: The Llano courses through limestone and sandstone canyons, where raptor life abounds. The San Marcos flows through farmland and is lined with live oaks and old-growth cypress trees. The Devils is perhaps the wildest river in Texas, running crystal clear through countryside that alternates between stark canyons and wooded hillsides. Though the Guadalupe River, also in the region, is the southernmost river in the United States to support a trout fishery, it's the warmwater species that attract most visiting anglers—largemouth bass, smallmouth bass, and a fish peculiar to Texas, the Guadalupe bass.

Guadalupe bass are closely related to largemouth and spotted bass, though since they have evolved primarily in smaller streams, they do not attain largemouth sizes. The fish can be distinguished by a black, diamond-shaped pattern on the sides and stripes along the belly. Where largemouth tend to dwell in the slower, deeper water, Guadalupe bass prefer faster water, not unlike smallmouth; in fact, Guadalupe and smallmouth have interbred in some of the Guadalupe and Colorado river drainages, which encompass most of the Hill Country rivers. The resultant hybrid is an extremely aggressive fish that rushes to engulf a fly. (Biologists are concerned that future generations of Guadalupe bass are in danger thanks to the interbreeding.) Being endemic to the Hill Country and found only in Texas, Guadalupe bass gained the distinction of being the Lone Star State's official fish in 1989.

OPPOSITE: The crystalline, often intimate rivers of the Texas Hill Country are best fished from a canoe.

Whether you're finding official state fish or humble largemouth, much of the fishing on Hill Country rivers takes place from a canoe. "Canoes are the most versatile craft for Texas," Tim continued. "The maneuverability, coupled with the speed of a canoe, allow access to all the region's streams. During periods of low water, a canoe's ability to access longer stretches of river and maneuver through rock gardens is key. They also make for a quiet approach. We're not doing a lot of sight casting for the bass—mostly probing fishy-looking water with poppers and streamers." If the thought of fly casting from a canoe is unnerving, take heart—on guided trips, anglers sit in front and cast while your guide steers from the back . . . and you'll get out and wet wade the most promising riffles and pools. Bass are center stage for many visitors, but there's plenty of warmwater species variety. "On the Llano system, we'll sometimes walk the side channels to sight-fish for carp," Tim added. "You'll also likely have a chance to cast to Rio Grande cichlid, another endemic species.

"One of the five most memorable days of fishing I've ever had came on the Llano River," Tim continued, "though it did come with a cost: a disease called bass thumb. The affliction affects the epidermis on the distal phalanges after repeated releases of large-mouth and Guadalupe bass. Fishing with Johnny Quiroz, a photographer friend [who also does some guiding], I had a single yellow popper that I fished for the entire day. I must have released fifty fish. At the end of the day, Johnny inspected my thumb, which looked like it had been worked over with a belt sander. 'You have bass thumb,' he said.

"It's a malady that I wish I suffered from more often."

DESTINATION

41

TIM ROMANO is a fine arts photographer, managing editor of *Angling Trade*, photo editor at *The Flyfish Journal*, and a frequent contributor to *Field & Stream's* Fly Talk blog. He was formerly an editor with *Fly Fishing Trade* and *Wild on the Fly* magazines. Assignments have taken him to Alaska, Chile, New Zealand, Russia, and the Bahamas, to list just a few of his travels. Tim's artwork is part of the permanent collections at Lake Forest College, Photo Americas Portland, Instituto de Artes de Medellin, Colombia, and the University of Colorado, Boulder. In 2005, Tim founded Guide for the Gulf to benefit fly-fishing charter captains impacted by Hurricane Katrina. He earned the award for Cover Design Excellence from the College Designers Association and has many magazine covers to his credit. He lives in Boulder, Colorado.

If You Go

▶ **Prime Time:** Fishing is open year-round in Hill Country rivers. Most fish best in the spring and fall, though on some systems, fishing can be good through the summer.
▶ **Getting There:** The Texas Hill Country can be easily reached from either Austin or San Antonio, which are both served by many major carriers.
▶ **Accommodations:** When visiting the Hill Country, Tim often stays in the music and barbecue hub of Austin, and the Austin Convention & Visitors Bureau (888-463-0211; www.austintexas.org) outlines lodging options. If you're fishing on the Llano, Tim recommends Raye Carrington's (866-605-3100; www.llanoriver.com), a B&B right on the banks.
▶ **Guides/Outfitters:** Johnny Quiroz and Marcus Rodriguez (956-802-1157/512-665-3261; www.guidesoftexas.com) guide on the region's rivers. Davis Fly Fishing Guide Service (512-557-4128; www.flyfishthehillcountry.com) also knows the waters well.
▶ **Equipment:** A 5- or 6-weight rod rigged with floating line will work for most situations. Poppers, Woolly Buggers, crayfish, and baitfish patterns will all work.

LAGUNA MADRE

RECOMMENDED BY **Eric Glass**

The backwater marshes of Louisiana may have less spooky redfish. The open water off Cape Lookout in North Carolina—especially in the fall—may have bigger redfish. But the protected waters of Laguna Madre in south Texas may be America's best venue to sight-fish for redfish. "We have great expanses of shallow, clear water, grass and sand flats, and a large variety of game fish," Captain Eric Glass said. "When you put them all together, you have something special."

Laguna Madre is a 300-square-mile lagoon, stretching 50 miles north from the southernmost tip of South Padre Island; it's the largest hypersaline lagoon system in the country. The lagoon has a maximum depth of 7 feet and an average depth of 3 feet, which helps explain its possibilities as a sight-fishing fishery. Though South Padre, on its eastern edge, sees its share of visitors (especially during college spring break), much of the Laguna Madre is a National Wildlife Refuge or National Seashore, hence protected from development. The western shore is covered with thickets of mesquite, yucca, and prickly pear, providing a backdrop that might seem more fitting for Arizona than the Gulf Coast.

Redfish are the bread and butter for guides and anglers alike on Laguna Madre. The lagoon serves as nursery for younger fish before they head out to deeper water in the Gulf of Mexico. "We have large numbers of one-and-a-half- to three-year-old fish, mostly in the 19- to 25-inch category," Eric described. "Many days we'll start on the grass and clay flats near the mainland on the west side. We'll often find tailing fish in areas like that. They can be in singles and pairs, small groups of four to six or big groups of fifty or more fish. As the sun gets high and the wind comes up in late morning, I like to move to some big white sand flats toward the center of the lagoon. The wind creates a little current, which can get the fish moving and feeding. These look more like bonefish flats than your typical

DESTINATION

42

187

redfish flats. When we come upon cruising reds, I like to drop the fly in a fish's path and let it sit until the fish gets close. I give the fly one strip to get the fish's attention, one more to make it pounce, and watch closely for the eat.

"Naturally colored crab and shrimp imitations work fine. South Texas redfish have a reputation for being challenging. I think they often exhibit a nice level of difficulty, but you're not going to have your hat handed to you by six fish in a row. If an angler has a good cast and we have average to good conditions, she should be able to land eight to ten fish in a full day of fishing. There have been days when we've boated more than fifty reds."

Though anglers may set out in search of redfish, opportunities to cast for other species often present themselves. Throughout the year one can search for snook, blind casting around creek mouths or piers. In the summer, they will appear on the flats. "It's not unlike the odds you find permit fishing," Eric said. "You're probably not going to see tons of snook on the flats, but there are enough of them around to present a legitimate target." Other fish found on the flats include black drum, sheepshead, ladyfish, and jack crevalle. "We take advantage of calm conditions from late spring through fall to fish for tarpon around Brazos Santiago Pass and along the beachfront," Eric added. "We encounter rolling fish, daisy chains, and laid-up fish as well. These tarpon range in size from 15 to 130 pounds, with most between 30 and 70 pounds. This fishery is extremely sensitive to nearshore sea conditions and is not an everyday option."

One of the thrills of fishing Laguna Madre is that you'll likely have a chance to sight cast to spotted sea trout—and you might drop a fly in front of a world-record "speck." Indeed, five current IGFA tippet-class world-record sea trout have been landed from Laguna Madre. (Spotted sea trout are not related to salmonids, though the black spots on their backs can be reminiscent of brown trout. They are close cousins to redfish.) "The specks move out into the lagoon in the summer, and that's when we see the most and the biggest trout," Eric said. "They can go as large as 15 pounds. There's an interesting phenomenon that I've seen on a few occasions in the summertime—tailing sea trout. Stingrays will move along the bottom feeding. As they stir up the sand, the sea trout come right behind them. It's like bonefishing, except you're in south Texas."

ERIC GLASS has been a full-time flats guide on the lower Laguna Madre for almost twenty years. He's been an avid angler since early childhood and enjoys trout and steelhead fishing when he's not on the flats. Eric has been featured in many publications,

OPPOSITE: Laguna Madre redfish aren't as big as their Louisiana brethren, but shallow, clear water provides ideal sight-fishing conditions.

DESTINATION

42

including *Saltwater Fly Fishing, Fly Fishing in Saltwaters, Field & Stream*, and *Fly Fish America*. He serves on the pro staff for Scott Fly Rod Company and Maverick Boat Company, and is an advisory board member of the Snook Foundation, a past board member of Port Isabel/South Padre Island Guides Association, and a board member of the Laguna Madre Fly Fishing Association.

If You Go

► **Prime Time:** Laguna Madre can fish well throughout the year. Eric's favorite time for redfish is April through November, though clear winter days can be outstanding.

► **Getting There:** Most visitors fly into the Brownsville/South Padre Island Airport, which is served by American Airlines (800-433-7300; www.aa.com) and Continental Airlines (800-523-3273; www.continental.com).

► **Accommodations:** The Redfish Inn (956-761-2722; www.redfishinn.com) is on the water and caters to anglers. Other accommodations are highlighted by the South Padre Island CVB (800-767-2373; www.sopadre.com).

► **Guides/Outfitters:** Several fly-fishing guides work Laguna Madre, including Eric Glass (956-434-1422; www.captainericglass.com) and Dale Fridy (956-345-5173; www.captainfridy.com).

► **Equipment:** For most circumstances, a 7- or 8-weight outfitted with floating line will suffice; a 10-weight with an intermediate and fast-sinking line will prepare you for tarpon, deeper water snook, king mackerel, and cobia. Guides will provide flies; if you want to tie your own, Eric recommends a collection of Tim Borski's bonefish flies.

LOS ROQUES

RECOMMENDED BY **Joel La Follette**

"There are three things that make Los Roques my favorite bonefishing destination," Joel La Follette began. "First, you have the potential for big fish. The fish there are all good quality, averaging 4 pounds or better, but there are many fish in the 10-pound range as well. Second, you often find tailing fish at Los Roques. There are many shallow flats that the fish love to push up on at high tides, and they feed aggressively. Third, Los Roques has a great variety of bonefish terrain—and it's nearly all wade fishing. You have the muddy flats typical of the Yucatán, the pancake flats one associates with Christmas Island, coral flats, marl-covered flats, turtle grass flats, and almost everything in between. Since you're wading, you're fishing all the time; there's no waiting for your angling partner to take her shot while you sit in the boat."

Los Roques is a coral atoll of a dozen sizable islands and hundreds of smaller islands and cays, all resting 80 miles north of Caracas, Venezuela . . . and 12 degrees north of the equator. This latter fact is of great significance, as it gives Los Roques extremely consistent weather—hence, consistent bonefishing conditions—throughout the year. "The conditions are truly ideal," Joel continued. "You're south of the hurricane belt, and you don't get the cold fronts that can come through Belize and Caribbean Mexico in the winter. Some clients I've talked to about Los Roques have been nervous about visiting thanks to President Chávez and his saber rattling. I tell them that Chávez is on the mainland, and you won't see him out on Los Roques. The only thing to worry about at Los Roques is the tides."

And it's those flats—varied and seemingly endless—that make Los Roques a dream come true, especially for bonefishers who enjoy a long stroll. "I recall one time fishing with a dear friend, Dr. Keith Hansen," Joel added. "We got onto a flat that was 3 or 4 miles long and 300 yards wide, with a mangrove berm blocking the wind. The water was ankle

to knee deep. Keith went off with the guide, and I fished behind them with a mantis shrimp pattern. The fish came in singles and doubles all morning. I had to make fairly technical casts, and it was very satisfying. Keith and the guide would turn around from time to time, and every time they did, I had a fish on. When I caught up with Keith, he said, 'Looks like you're catching a lot of fish.' Normally I don't count fish, but this morning I did: eighteen."

At some bonefish venues, a handful of time-tested bonefish patterns—Gotchas, Bonefish Charlies, Christmas Island Specials—will likely do the trick. At Los Roques, anglers will do well to expand their repertoire. "The archipelago is just teeming with glass minnows, forage fish that are about 2.5 inches long," Joel said. "The bones really focus on them at times, and a lot of anglers like to use something called a Gummy Minnow. I tied up a glass minnow pattern with epoxy that I like a little better. The fish also go for crabs more than I've witnessed in other places. The crab flies at Los Roques have to be lighter, as the flats are shallow. I came up with one pattern I called the Louie Louie Crab, with a beige body and orange rubber legs. The guides shook their heads when I took it out, but it caught fish. Before I left, one of the guides who had initially disliked the fly bashfully asked if I could leave him some of my crabs."

Thanks to the extensive flats, your fishing crew at Los Roques consists of one guide and one boatman per vessel. This way, the guide and anglers can be picked up after they've fished a flat instead of walking back over ground they've covered. The memory of one of Los Roques' boatman will likely stay with Joel for years to come. "The boatman on my raft during one visit—a young man named Carlos—happened to be deaf and mute. He was excellent at handling the boat, but he never guided, due to his lack of speech. When we reached a flat that was out by the barrier reef, I sent my friend Troy off with the guide. But before they began wading, I asked if it would be okay for Carlos to go with me. The guide shrugged his shoulders and said, 'Sure. But he can't speak.' They went off down the flat, and Carlos and I started in the other direction. There was an incredible amount of noise and stimulation out there—birds squawking, waves crashing on the reef. I couldn't help but wonder if Carlos could somehow feel this, even if he couldn't hear it.

"I soon saw some fish coming toward us, but I didn't show that I saw them; I wanted to see if Carlos spotted them. He saw them very soon after and pointed enthusiastically. I dropped a cast in and hooked a fish. We high-fived. Over the next hour, we landed three more. When we caught up with Troy and the guide, we learned that they hadn't caught

OPPOSITE:
Los Roques is
for walkers—
productive flats
of all types
stretch for miles.

any. Carlos thumped the other guide in the chest and held up four fingers. The joy he had in having one-upped the guide was irrepressible.

"It's common practice to leave some flies or extra pairs of shoes with your guides at the end of a trip, as such items are hard to come by in a place like Los Roques. When we got off the boat the last day, I tossed Carlos my flats pack. He thought I wanted him to carry it to the beach, but I made it clear that I wanted him to have it. He strapped it right on. That night, walking around through town, I felt a tug on my arm. It was Carlos, wanting to greet me. He was still wearing the flats pack."

JOEL LA FOLLETTE learned the art of fly fishing in the cool pine forest along the banks of the Metolius River at the ripe old age of nine. His grandfather had brought him there to share some of the joys of his childhood on that same stream. Since that first outing, Joel has fished the wilds of Belize, Mexico, the Bahamas, Christmas Island, and of course Los Roques for bonefish, tarpon, permit, trevally, and other saltwater fishes. He's traveled the northeast for brookies, browns, and stripers, and has chased steelhead in British Columbia. After an adventurous career that has included working as a commercial fisherman, professional photographer, and race car driving instructor, Joel has been in the fly-fishing industry for more than fourteen years and has recently opened his own fly shop, Royal Treatment Fly Fishing (www.royaltreatmentflyfishing.com) in West Linn, Oregon.

If You Go

▶ **Prime Time:** Though weather conditions are ideal year-round, tides are optimal from mid-January through September.

▶ **Getting There:** Los Roques is reached via Caracas, Venezuela, which is served by most major international carriers: A charter flight will take you to Gran Roque.

▶ **Accommodations/Outfitter:** Fly-fishing adventures at Los Roques are orchestrated by Sight Cast (+58 212 277 3312; www.sightcast.org) and can be booked through many fly-fishing booking agents.

▶ **Equipment:** A 7- or 8-weight rod with floating line and at least 150 yards of backing will suffice. A list of preferred flies resides at www.royaltreatmentflyfishing.com.

RIVERS TEIFI AND TOWY

RECOMMENDED BY **Steffan Jones**

"If you're born in Scotland and are a fly fisher, you remember your first Atlantic salmon," Steffan Jones opined. "If you're born in Wales, you remember your first sea trout. Sea trout are a large part of the angling culture, a religion of sorts. One pull of sea trout in the dark transforms your understanding of fly fishing. It's a drug to those who pursue it."

The sea trout (*sewin* in Welsh) that return to the rivers of Wales (and those of Ireland, Scotland, and England) may be unfamiliar to anglers from across the pond. Though genetically identical to brown trout, their life cycle is quite different. They are an anadromous species, spending their early days in the river, swimming out to sea during their adult phase to feed, and returning to the sweet water to propagate. Unlike salmon, most fish will return to the salt for another cycle. Unlike their other anadromous cousins, sea-runs do not range far afield once reaching the salt of the Irish Sea. Instead, they prowl the coastlines, feeding on baitfish, sand eels, and crustaceans. The fish spawn in late fall and winter, but begin returning to their natal streams as early as March, with runs concentrated in the rivers by summer. Upon their return to the river, sea-runs are bright silver, hence a nickname used by some anglers—the silver tourists.

Many of the rivers that feed into the Irish Sea are home to sea trout, among them the Dyfi, the Mawddach, the Rheidol, the Ystwyth, and the Conwy. For aficionados like Steffan Jones, two stand out—the Teifi and the Towy, both in the region of West Wales. "The Teifi is the Queen of Welsh Rivers," he continued. "It's a classic freestone river, not a huge gradient, but a fairly stiff flow; it puts more water into the sea than the Thames, though it's only a third as wide. If you fish a pool, you can see the head and tail in one glance. It's not renowned for huge fish—a 4- to 6-pound specimen would be a very decent fish—but the numbers are good, with 2,000 to 3,000 sea trout taken each year. All the fish are wild.

The Towy is just thirty minutes away, but it's worlds apart. It's more of a lowland-type river, meandering rather than crashing and tumbling. It's perhaps not as interesting a system in terms of its surroundings and structure, but there's no equal for big fish; a 22-pounder was taken in 2008, and I've had an outing when I've seen four double-figure fish caught on one beat."

The rolling hills and verdant pastureland of West Wales is quite charming, but don't expect to take in too much while chasing sea trout. That's because serious sea trouting takes place in the wee hours of the night. "I like to say that we fish the hours of the vampire, from ten at night until four in the morning," Steffan continued. "As ardent anglers we should have bronze skin, but you can always tell sea trout fishermen by their pale complexions. Attention is focused on night fishing because the trout are most active at night. Their experience at sea has conditioned them this way, as sand eels are more active at night, and that's an important sea trout forage. Even though the sea trout are not feeding in the river, they're still in a nighttime frame of mind." (*Note:* as tempting as it might be to enjoy a pint or two of fine Welsh ales, Steffan warns against it—"You'll be asleep by midnight.")

There are nuances to night fishing, though Steffan pointed out that all is predicated on an understanding of river craft. "It pays to do a little reconnaissance during the daytime," he continued, "walking the beat[s] you'll be fishing, even doing some wading so you can scout the drop-offs. It's very important to wait until it's properly dark before you begin fishing. Properly dark is not sunset, but when you cannot make out the foliage across the river; otherwise, you will spook the fish. Ideally, you'll have a mild cloudy evening. If it's clear and cool, mist will develop on the river—we call it tarth. When the tarth comes on, you call it a night, as not enough light penetrates the water, and the sea trout can't see your offerings. Your vision acclimatizes surprisingly well to nighttime conditions, though feeling is more important than seeing. You always want to feel your fly, especially as the fish swipe at it quickly. I like to use a 10-foot, 8-weight rod with medium action. A fast-action rod creates tight loops, and at night, that can create tangles. The fish have soft mouths, too, and with a softer rod, you're less likely to pull the hook out."

An evening's fishing will generally go like this. You'll arrive at your beat before nightfall for an inspection. If there are riffles, it may be permissible to fish those before darkness is complete. When you begin fishing in earnest, Steffan recommends starting with a team of two small flies—1 inch long at most. As night progresses, you may go to

OPPOSITE:
A night on the River Towy nears conclusion. "You can recognize sea trout anglers by their pale complexion," Steffan Jones quips.

DESTINATION

44

progressively larger flies, up to 4 inches (tube flies are popular). "If you're not sure where to fish, the sea trout will often make their presence known with splashy surface rolls," Steffan explained. "How you present the fly will depend on the current. In faster water, you'll cast downstream and make a slower retrieve; in slower water, you'll cast across the current and make a quicker retrieve. On an average evening, you'll fish the same one or two pools several times, varying your tactics as you go through. While presentation is important, a level of confidence that a fish *will* grab is imperative. Some fantastic daytime anglers have a lot of trouble at night until they've built up their confidence."

STEFFAN JONES began guiding on the sea trout rivers of West Wales when he was fifteen and still guides there today. He also owns and operates Angling Worldwide, which organizes and leads fly-fishing trips around Wales and to Chile, Argentina, Cuba, and beyond. Steffan also oversees Frontiers International's sea trout program. He spends each summer fishing and guiding on his home waters. His writing and photography can often be seen gracing the pages of fishing publications in the UK and other countries. See his work at www.sea-trout.co.uk and www.sportingimagery.com.

If You Go

▶ **Prime Time:** The season runs from early spring until October, but fresh fish are present in the greatest numbers from June through August.

▶ **Getting There:** Wales is served from the U.S.A. by Aer Lingus (800-474-7424; www .aerlingus.com). Some will opt to fly into London and take Britrail (www.britrail.com) to Wales.

▶ **Accommodations:** The Fishing Wales website (www.fishing.visitwales.com) lists a variety of accommodations.

▶ **Guides/Outfitters:** Angling Worldwide (+44 559 364 999; www.anglingworldwide .com) guides on many Welsh rivers, including the Teifi and Towy. Fishing Wales (www .fishing.visitwales.com) can help you secure a beat if you opt to go it alone.

▶ **Equipment:** Steffan recommends a medium-action 8-weight rod outfitted with a float-ing line and an intermediate sinking line. Your guide (or the syndicate that manages the beat you lease) will have fly suggestions.

MIDDLE POTOMAC RIVER

RECOMMENDED BY **Mike Bailey**

Springtime in Washington, DC: cherry blossoms are blooming, wide-eyed vacationing schoolchildren are walking the National Mall . . . and attorneys, lobbyists—and even the occasional highly placed legislator or government official—can be found sneaking off to Fletcher's Cove on the Potomac to cast for shad.

"Fletcher's Cove is just below the fall line—the point on the Potomac where there's no longer any tidal effect from the Atlantic," explained Mike Bailey. "It's a natural staging area for the American and hickory shad that return each year to spawn. The Fletcher's Cove Boathouse has been in existence here since the 1850s to cater to anglers. You can still come down, rent a skiff, and head out to fish one of the famous holes within 400 yards of the dock—The Shelf, Forked Tree, Drapers Rock, Boiling Rock, The Chute. I've been fishing around Fletcher's since the early eighties, and in that time I have watched the fishery develop from a marginal to poor fishery into something fantastic. I've also been able to witness the regrowth of fly fishing on the Potomac as the fishery has recovered."

A case can be made that shad are the quintessential American fish. In fact, John McPhee has elegantly argued said case in his fine title, *The Founding Fish*. George Washington, McPhee points out, was a commercial shad fisherman before taking the helm of the revolutionary forces and resignedly ascending to the presidency. The story of how the spring shad run on Pennsylvania's Schuylkill River saved the nascent United States army at Valley Forge in the winter of 1778 can be recited by almost every angler who's ever tossed a dart. McPhee mentions that "it would not have been a leap of the imagination for [Washington] to anticipate the spring shad run and choose a campsite accordingly." On a metaphoric level, the shad illustrate the spunk, tenacity, and egalitari-

DESTINATION

45

anism that Americans, at their best moments, display. American shad (*Alosa sapidissima*, Latin for "most delicious") average around 5 pounds and historically have returned to rivers from Florida to Nova Scotia; in the twentieth century, they were successfully introduced into several systems on the West Coast of the United States (where shad of up to 15 pounds have been landed). Shad are a member of the herring family; the sobriquet "poor man's tarpon" is not inaccurate, at least from a genus/species perspective . . . though another common descriptor, "poor man's salmon" also has some relevance, as like salmon, shad are born in freshwater, spend their adult years at sea, and return to their natal stream to spawn and die.

Shad helped sustain Native Americans along the Potomac for countless generations, and in turn early English settlers. By the 1950s, however, runs that had been in the millions had been decimated. "It was a combination of the effects of overfishing downriver by commercial fishermen and pollution coming from industry and municipalities upriver," Mike continued. "Since that time, the Interstate Commission on the Potomac River Basin has dedicated considerable resources to improving water quality, creating fish ladders, and spearheading other habitat restoration efforts. Moratoriums were also placed on commercial fishing. The Potomac River American Shad Restoration Project was launched by the ICPRB in 1995, in cooperation with many regional agencies, to rejuvenate the runs through an intensive stocking program. All these initiatives have combined to create a great urban fishery success story."

Shad are an integral link in the Potomac's larger ecosystem. Where they can be harvested, they're considered a treat. As much to the point for anglers: they're fun to catch. Shad take a fly with gusto, they fight hard, and if you find one, you'll likely find more.

"Fly fishing for shad is quite different than trout fishing," Mike opined. "In fact, it's about as close to set line fishing as you can get with a fly rod. When the fish return, they collect en masse in river pockets and go into a holding pattern before they decide to push on. To fish them effectively around Fletcher's Cove, you position your boat so you can work a seam as the tide comes in or goes out. Long casts are not critical, but having a sinking line or at least a sinking leader is important. A very slow retrieve is also essential. You want to keep the fly in the zone where the fish are staging as long as possible. It's much more of a wrist action then an elbow action. Flies in red or chartreuse green work best. A little flashabou to give the fly a shrimp- or crustacean-like appearance seems to help. Some people will use two flies or a fly and a dart in tandem. With this sort of rig, it's pretty common to get double hook-ups. It's a pretty forgiving fishery—if your fly or dart is in the water at the right depth and the fish come through, you're going to get some."

Shad excitement on the Potomac reaches an apex late each April with the Jim Range National Casting Call. This event, hosted by the American Fly Fishing Trade Association (and highlighting the conversation efforts of the National Fish Habitat Action Plan), brings both seasoned and first-time anglers to the Potomac to catch shad and appreciate the possibilities of collaborative fisheries management. "The Casting Call is as much a social event as a fishing event," Mike said. "Boats are cozied up next to each other so people can chat and fish at the same time. I would venture to say that a number of important decisions regarding habitat restoration that have been *contemplated* at the office are *made* in the boat. I'd be the first to admit that if you can get a legislator out to fish, you can perhaps sway certain legislative decisions . . . especially if the fishing is good!"

Jim Range was a passionate advocate of fisheries habitat restoration (as well as a passionate fly angler) and worked from the inside as a lobbyist for a powerful law firm to help bring about change. Mike still recalls his first meeting with Jim—fittingly enough, at Fletcher's Cove Boathouse. "It was 1996, and Joe Fletcher was still around. My nickname is Animal, and Joe said, 'Animal, take this guy fishing.' I said okay, and we got in the boat. I asked Jim what he did, and he said, 'I'm a lawyer and a lobbyist.' He had a fly rod and spinning rod in hand, and we headed out in the rain. We fished for eight straight hours in a downpour and caught hundreds of shad—no stopping for food or bathroom breaks. That was my real introduction to fly fishing and fish habitat restoration. Jim was committed to making sure that we—and our children and grandchildren—have a place to fish. I'm retired now and helping work toward his dream."

MIKE BAILEY is avid angler—fly and conventional gear—and an ambassador for the Jim Range National Casting Call. In this capacity, he works to promote fish habitat restoration and youth fishing. A Maryland resident and seasoned Potomac River angler, Mike has fished for fresh and saltwater species worldwide. Mike cofounded the Automated Weather Source, now known as WeatherBug, and the success of that business has enabled him to focus more on building awareness for fishing and fish habitat restoration.

DESTINATION

45

If You Go

► **Prime Time:** Shad begin arriving in the Lower Potomac in late March and are present through late May, though the season is at its peak in April—around the time of the Jim Range National Casting Call.

► **Getting There:** Fletcher's Cove is within the city limits of Washington, DC, a few miles upstream of Georgetown and Reagan National Airport.

► **Accommodations:** Destination DC (800-422-8644; http://washington.org) lists lodging options around the U.S. capital.

► **Guides/Outfitters:** While no guides work the Potomac regularly, the folks at Urban Angler in Arlington (800-800-2018; www.urbanangler.com) can provide guidance, as can the staff at Fletcher's Cove Boathouse (202-244-0461; www.fletcherscove.com). Preregistered guests can participate in the Jim Range National Casting Call (www .nationalcastingcall.com), where you'll receive plenty of guidance and encouragement.

► **Equipment:** A 5- or 6-weight rod outfitted with a sink-tip or full sinking line is ideal for shad fishing on the Potomac. Flies (or darts, small enough to be cast) in red or chartreuse dressed with a little flashabou work well. The boathouse stocks popular patterns.

QUEETS RIVER

RECOMMENDED BY **Mike Dickson**

Readers of *Twilight* novels know, there are scary things, monsters, really, lurking in the deep woods of the Olympic Peninsula. Anglers like Mike Dickson know the identity of those monsters, and where they can be found—they are native steelhead, and each winter they come home to haunt the region's perpetually mist-enshrouded rivers, like the Queets. "You can fish year-round for steelhead on the Olympic Peninsula, but there's a specific time frame when the big wild fish appear," Mike offered. "That's usually February, March, and April. When your fly stops in the middle of the swing, you know it could be a monster fish, the steelhead of a lifetime."

The Olympic Peninsula rests on the northwestern edge of the continental United States. The river valleys here have a remnant of what was once the greatest temperate rain forest in the world; it's a veritable museum piece for trees, holding the "biggest tree" found anywhere for a variety of western species. Sitka spruce and western hemlock dominate the landscape, but western red cedar, Douglas fir, and Engelmann spruce, among other conifers, are also present. Some of the largest specimens can approach 60 or 70 feet in circumference and reach heights of more than 250 feet. Almost as impressive are the mosses, ferns, and lichens that spring from the trunks of these giants. Even in the less-than-bright light that's the norm most of the year, the tangle of greens on display is so varied that they'd make the color namers at Sherwin-Williams jump for joy. Still, if there's a defining feature of the Olympic Peninsula, it is water—the 135 inches of rain that fall on average in the Queets River basin, the more than 50 feet of snow that accumulates on Mount Olympus, and the three thousand miles of rivers and creeks that radiate from the park's central mountains, hosting healthy runs of salmon and steelhead and acting as a circulatory system for Olympic National Park's varied ecosystems.

DESTINATION

46

The Queets is the second largest watershed on the peninsula. Beginning in the glaciers of Mount Olympus, it cascades through box canyons and violent rapids in its upper reaches before arriving at the rain forest and ultimately the Pacific. Nearly all the 51-mile-long river lies in Olympic National Park, with its final few miles flowing through the Quinault Indian Reservation. In its lower 20 miles, where much of the fishing occurs, the Queets is typified by wide flood plains, immense gravel bars, and intimidating logjams, with root wads reaching high into the sky. "On the Queets, you have a sense that you're in a 'last frontier' kind of area," Mike continued. "It's a freestone river, it's not very developed, and there's the rain forest—the immense trees everywhere. On the Puget Sound steelhead rivers like the Stillaguamish and Skykomish, you don't have a wilderness feeling. On the Queets, you can get away to spots where you won't see other people, if you put your nose to it." Another constant of the Queets is low visibility. "It's always fairly dirty water," Mike added, "thanks to its glacial origins. The maximum visibility I've seen on the river is 4 feet, though 2 to 3 feet is more common . . . and I've hooked plenty of fish when there's only 18 inches of visibility, or even less. When you have dirty water, fish will pull into softer seams, and into shallower, slower water. They'll hang in closer—they're not playing hide-and-seek. If you get the fly close, the fish take aggressively, they don't ask questions. I'd much rather have off-color water and dark conditions. Bright day and clearer water are the toughest."

The Queets is one of the last strongholds of wild steelhead in Washington State. Returns of winter fish have approached twelve thousand on good years. (Winter steelhead enter their natal rivers in a sexually mature state; they tend to spawn fairly quickly upon arrival. Summer steelhead enter rivers sexually immature and don't spawn until the winter, sometimes spending six months or more in the freshwater.) Steelhead aficionados find special appeal in these winter fish—dubbed "ghosts" by some—with their monochrome flanks with nary a blush of magenta on their gill plates. These winter steelhead bear little resemblance to their genetic doubles, rainbow trout. Then there's the size of Queets fish. "We'll get several fish in the 20-pound range every season," Mike said. "The average winter fish are 10 to 14 pounds. I was chatting with a Quinault lady one day, and she showed me a picture of a 35-pound fish that some guy had caught on the Quinault River. There's no doubt that you have a shot at big fish like that in the Queets—and for that matter, the other rivers on the peninsula. Even though the water is cold, these fish put up a good fight. They'll run hard and often jump. That's why these

OPPOSITE:
Big trees—and
potential for very
big steelhead—
bring anglers
to the Olympic
Peninsula
and the Queets
each winter.

DESTINATION

46

fish are so sought after. They aren't easy to catch, but I think the Queets has easier wading than the other rivers, and there's lots of backcasting room. On a lot of the runs, the fish are going to be within 40 feet of where you're standing, so you don't have to throw a lot of line. Still, a spey rod is helpful to have, as it makes throwing heavy sink tips and weighted flies easier."

Given that the Olympic Peninsula is the wettest place in the Lower 48, and that the Queets is one of the wettest places on the peninsula, there are times when the Queets will get too high to be fishable. Unless you have a penchant for vampire trivia, it pays to be flexible when winter steelheading. "It's a very dynamic region to fish, and we have to let conditions dictate where we go," Mike explained. "All the rivers will blow out at times, but it takes quite a bit of rain in a brief period for everything to blow out. There are six good rivers within an hour's drive, and they all have a different feeling. The Queets is usually one of the first to go out. The Hoh hangs in there a little longer. The Bogachiel lasts longer than the Hoh, though since it's closer to Forks, it gets more traffic. I like the Clearwater, though it's a little more technical and requires heavier tips and flies. The Sol Duc is one of the last rivers to go out completely, but it doesn't have as much good swinging water; you might have to use an indicator more there."

You may not get a 20-pounder on the Queets, but you're pretty sure to get some rain. "We're so close to the Pacific, the weather is constantly changing," Mike added. "Plus, you're fishing in a rain forest. You have to dress for everything and hope for the best. If you're not out in it, you can be pretty sure you won't catch anything."

MIKE DICKSON grew up fly fishing in his hometown of Arlington, Washington, where he has been guiding since the age of eighteen. He has been a full-time guide since 2000, working with his father, Dennis Dickson. Steelhead are Mike's primary focus, and in addition to the rivers of the Olympic Peninsula, he guides on the Skagit, the Skykomish, the Cowlitz, and the Grande Ronde, among others. He also leads annual trips to the Caribbean to focus on tarpon. Mike is the owner-operator of Dickson's virtual fly shop (www.streamsideflyshop.com), where he and his father have developed their own line of fly-fishing equipment, lines, and flies.

If You Go

▶ **Prime Time:** Steelhead are present in the system year-round, but the big winter fish show up in March and April.

▶ **Getting There:** The closest major airport is Sea-Tac Airport, which is served by most major carriers; it's roughly four hours' drive to the settlement of Kalaloch, on the western edge of the park.

▶ **Accommodations:** Kalaloch Lodge (866-525-2562; www.visitkalaloch.com) offers cozy cabins a short drive from the Queets. The Olympic Peninsula Tourist Commission (www .olympicpeninsula.org) highlights lodging options outside the park, including in Forks.

▶ **Guides/Outfitters:** Dickson Fly Fishing Guides (425-330-9506; www.flyfishsteelhead .com) leads trips on the Queets and other OP rivers. Emerald Water Anglers (206-545-2197; www.emeraldwateranglers.com) also leads Queets trips.

▶ **Equipment:** Many prefer spey rods for the sink tips and heavy flies the Queets may call for, but long casts are not always necessary. Whether single- or double-hand, an 8- to 9-weight outfit with sink tips ranging from type 6 to type 14 will suffice. Mike is not particular about fly color or style, though he feels they need a large profile—at least 3 inches. Bring weighted and unweighted patterns.

PUGET SOUND

RECOMMENDED BY **Dave McCoy**

East of the Cascade Mountains, the state of Washington offers some fine trout fishing. *OPPOSITE:*
The Yakima River, the Pothole Lakes, and Rocky Ford Creek all have their attractions and *The quest for*
proponents. But for Dave McCoy, the Evergreen State's greatest trout bounty lies west of *sea-run cutthroats*
the mountains; in fact, it rests in the salt, in the shape of sea-run cutthroats. *unfolds amid*

"Puget Sound is unique in the northern part of our hemisphere," Dave began. *the suburban*
"Thanks to the landmass of the Olympic Peninsula to the west, you have a saltwater fish- *(and sometimes*
ery that's shielded from the rough conditions the ocean can bring. You get all the benefits *urban) environs*
of a rich saltwater environment—including resident whales, porpoises, and several fly *of Puget Sound.*
rod species—without crashing surf and stomach-turning swells. I first fished for sea-runs
while visiting my grandma as a teenager. When I moved back to Seattle in 1999 with
plans to open a guiding business, I went fishing for them with a fly shop owner in town.
I quickly realized that this was going to be one of my primary fisheries. A lot of the fly
shop owners in the region thought I was an idiot, that no one would be interested in
guided trips on Puget Sound. Today, it's 60 percent of my business."

Puget Sound encompasses more than 1,000 square miles of water and 2,500 miles of
coastline, stretching from the city of Olympia in the south to Port Townsend and Whidbey
Island in the north. Much of Washington's population—some four million souls—live
along or near Puget Sound, including the residents of Seattle and Tacoma. The sound is
hardly pristine; the combined ports of Tacoma and Seattle are the second busiest in the
country, and many heavy industries operate along its shores. Still, with the inflow from
ten thousand creeks and rivers to dilute some of the effluents that reach the sound, and
the tidal influence of the Strait of Juan de Fuca to inject nutrients into the system, Puget
Sound supports a healthy population of marine life . . . including the sea-runs.

Sea-run cutthroat—also known as coastal cutthroat, bluebacks, or their formal name, *Salmo clarki clarki*—range from the streams and estuaries of northern California to the waters of the Inside Passage off southeast Alaska. Sea-runs can range in size from 10 to 24 inches, though fish exceeding 20 inches are considered trophy size. When the fish visit the salt or the sweet—and how much time they spend in these respective environments—varies depending on the region, though most agree that the sea-run's life cycle mirrors that of a steelhead. "While few scientific studies have been conducted, I would surmise that the fish spend their first year in the river, and the rest of their time in the salt, with returns to their natal river to spawn," Dave continued. "It's believed that at least sixteen rivers in the Puget Sound provide spawning habitat, though there seems to be some variance when the fish spawn. You'll catch one fish that's chrome bright with sea lice clinging to its sides, its namesake slash marks nearly invisible. Your next fish might be yellow and gold and with prominent cuts, like a fish that's only lived in freshwater." Both are quite beautiful.

While the physical appearance of Puget Sound cutts may vary, their willingness to take a well-presented fly is consistently strong, much like their mountain stream brethren when presented with a high-riding attractor pattern. Sea-runs tend to be found within casting distance of shoreline, in water less than 10 feet deep—though finding them can present a challenge given all that shoreline. "You can fish for sea-runs from a boat, but I prefer to fish from the beach," Dave said. "When you're on terra firma, you're able to get a better grasp of what's going on with the current, and it's also easier to get a sense of what the fish might be eating. You certainly can catch fish by tying on a Clouser, the Humpy of the saltwater world, but that won't make you a better angler. I like to match the hatch as much as possible—whether its chum salmon fry or sand lances or marine worms. On a given day, we may visit anywhere from two to six or eight beaches. Where we start will depend on the tides; it's most productive to stay on the lee side. We begin early, as most of the forage that the cutts feed on rely on microlife that's light sensitive and descends deeper into the water column as the sun comes up. I advise anglers to start with short casts, giving out more line until they reach a comfortable casting distance. Once you have an amount of line out, cast down current, parallel to the beach. You'll use different sorts of strips depending on what bait you're trying to imitate. If you don't find anything after working a stretch of beach, it's probably time to try a new location. The fish are moving, and if you stand in the same spot, it's like waiting for lightning to strike."

It may take a few stops to find the fish, but once you're on them, you'll know it. "More often than not, you'll find yourself casting to rolling or jumping cutts," Dave added. "At such times, they're not terrifically selective—some call them dumb, but I like to think of them as opportunistic. When the fish are on the surface, they'll take a Titanic Slider, and you get to see the whole episode play out in front of you. Sometimes they'll tail swat or slash at the fly before they take the Slider. The cutts will really jolt a 5- or 6-weight. An 18-inch fish is a fun play on such tackle—a fish in the 20s can be like fighting a fresh steelhead."

DAVE MCCOY began fishing as a boy in Eugene, Oregon; as every single person in his family fly fished, he had no choice in the matter! Today he owns and operates Emerald Water Anglers, a fly-fishing outfitter based in Seattle. His angling adventures have taken him from the steelhead rivers of the Pacific Northwest to Central America, the Caribbean, India, Tierra del Fuego, Mongolia, the South Pacific, and beyond. Dave serves on the pro staffs of Winston, Bauer, Rajeff Sports, among other manufacturers, and is an FFF-certified casting instructor. In addition to a busy guiding schedule, Dave is an avid photographer. You can view his work at http://davemccoyphotography.com.

If You Go

▶ **Prime Time:** Cutthroat fishing in Puget Sound can be good year-round, though different parts of the sound fish better at different times of year.

▶ **Getting There:** Most major carriers serve Sea-Tac Airport.

▶ **Accommodations:** The Seattle Convention and Visitors Bureau (206-461-5888; www.visitseattle.org) outlines lodging options in the greater Seattle area.

▶ **Guides/Outfitters:** Emerald Water Anglers (206-545-2197; www.emeraldwateranglers.com) and Sound Fly Fishing (206-940-3020; www.soundflyfishing.com).

▶ **Equipment:** A 5- or 6-weight rod outfitted with floating or intermediate sinking lines will work for most situations. Local fly shops can recommend popular patterns.

DESTINATION 47

THE DRIFTLESS REGION

RECOMMENDED BY **Dr. Gary Borger**

What state has more than 10,000 miles of trout streams—including more than 4,000 miles that foster wild trout? The answer, Wisconsin, might be a surprise for those who think of lakes and loons, or muskie and walleye, when they ponder the Badger State. The focal point of Wisconsin trout fishing is a region that Dr. Gary Borger calls the Fertile Crescent—and that others call the Driftless Region. "The Fertile Crescent is topographically much different than the rest of Wisconsin, where you have rolling land, moraines, and pothole lakes," Gary explained. "This area was never glaciated. There are high limestone hills, sharp valleys, and rock cliffs. [In other words, it was spared the impact of glacial drift, hence is 'driftless.'] The rivers here have tremendous variety. Some flow through forested land, some through cow pastures. There are weed-choked spring creeks and sparkling brooks with classic riffle-pool structure. They have glassy surfaces that let you see fish, and the fish are up on the surface a lot."

The Driftless Region encompasses 24,000 square miles in southeast Minnesota, northeast Iowa, northwest Illinois, and southwest and west-central Wisconsin. A recent Trout Unlimited report identified more than 600 spring creeks (exceeding 4,000 river miles) in the region, with the lion's share flowing through Wisconsin. Thanks to its geological makeup, the Driftless Region has one of the highest concentrations of limestone spring creeks in the world, creeks that support native brook and wild brown and rainbow trout. Black Earth Creek, Mount Vernon Creek, Trout Creek, Coon Valley Creek, Castle Rock Creek, Rush Creek, Kinnickinnic River, Kickapoo River, and Willow River are just a few. Each of these fisheries has its own special characteristics. Yet, as Gary described, they are unified in offering a particular kind of angling experience: "In the Driftless area, there's as much hunting and stalking as there is casting. It's lighter tackle, very refined—

and, I would say, more challenging than the angling on your average freestone river. Your quarry is mostly brown trout, and they're wary. There are some big fish in these streams—25 inches and more. They're not readily available, and if you do hook one, you probably won't land it. But you'll sure have fun for a few minutes!"

It's next to impossible to visit all the creeks of southwest Wisconsin in one fishing season—let alone in one trip. Gary suggested making your way south to north or north to south to get a sampling. Beginning in the south, you could do worse than starting at Castle Rock Creek. Castle Rock meanders slowly through pasturelands. Its greenish tint hints at its fertility; indeed the creek is rich in vegetation that supports both crustacean and insect life. Castle Rock is renowned for its tremendous hatches—especially its Blue-Wing Olive emergence, which is often well under way by the time the season opens. "In March, there might still be 18 inches of snow on the ground," Gary said, "but you can still get a tremendous hatch of *Baetis*. I recall being there once and seeing thousands of little holes in the snow, as if someone had poked their finger in. Each one held a *Baetis*."

Next, you could opt to move to the northwest, paralleling the Mississippi River until you reach Coon Valley and Coon Creek, one of Wisconsin's most fertile brown trout fisheries. The creek's intimate upper reaches attract most angler attention. Here, it flows through thick woodlands and is fed by other small, but equally fecund streams—Bohemian Valley, Rudlands, and most notably, Timber Coulee Creek, which may have the greatest brown trout biomass in the state.

Farther north toward the town of Hudson, another collection of streams await. These include the Willow, the Eau Galle, the Kinnickinnic, and the Rush. Like other Driftless Region fisheries, these creeks are home primarily to brown trout, though brook trout—the only trout species native to Wisconsin—are also found here. The Rush has more of a freestone character than many Driftless streams, and has produced a fair share of browns more than 20 inches. The "Kinni" has been called the most productive trout stream in Upper Mississippi River Basin, with wild fish populations approaching an astounding 10,000 fish per mile in some stretches. Its upper reaches flow through meadow country, and here the Kinni has a typical spring creek character. Lower down, it rambles through a 200-foot-deep canyon, with more clearly defined riffles and pools.

"You could easily spend three or four days fishing from Castle Rock to Coon Valley to the Kinni and Willow," Gary mused. "Then again, you could easily spend three or four days fishing at each spot."

Dr. Gary Borger began fly fishing when he was ten years old, and began creating and fishing the most awful-looking flies that ever came off a tier's bench by age eleven; before he was twelve, he'd caught his first trout, a 10-inch rainbow, which is his most memorable trophy. After getting his MS at Penn State in 1968, Gary headed to the University of Wisconsin–Madison, to work on his PhD in tree physiology. He sold his first magazine article to *Field & Stream* in 1972, and published his first book, *Nymphing,* in 1979. This was followed by *Naturals* in 1981 and Gary's first video, *Nymphing,* produced with Mike Dry. The success of that video led to three more fly-fishing productions for the 3M Company shortly thereafter. Gary then formed Tomorrow River Press with his wife, Nancy, and published *Designing Trout Flies* in 1991 and *Presentation* in 1995. He also had the chance to be involved in the film adaptation of *A River Runs Through It.* Gary has been blessed to have fished on every continent expect Antarctica. As of this writing, Gary and his son, Jason, are working on a twenty-volume book series titled *Fly Fishing,* with volume one, *Fishing the Film,* published in 2010. For more information, visit www.garyborger.com.

If You Go

▶ **Prime Time:** The general trout season runs from early May through September, though some streams open for catch and release fishing on March 1.

▶ **Getting There:** The closest commercial airports are in Madison and La Crosse. Madison is served by many carriers, including American Airlines (800-433-7300; www.aa.com) and Continental Airlines (800-525-3273; www.continental.com). Lacrosse is served by American Airlines and Delta Airlines (800-221-1212; www.delta.com).

▶ **Accommodations:** The Driftless Region website (www.driftlesswisconsin.com) highlights many lodging options in the region.

▶ **Guides/Outfitters:** Driftless Angler (608-637-8779; www.driftlessangler.com) and Streamside Outfitters (608-295-6517; www.streamsideoutfitters.com) guide the region's rivers.

▶ **Equipment:** A short (8 feet or less) and light (3-weight to 5-weight) rod is best for the intimate rivers. The Driftless Angler and FlyFishingWis.com websites highlight common hatches.

GREATER HAYWARD

RECOMMENDED BY **Robert Tomes**

Every few years, a new sport fish emerges as the "it" species for fly fishers to target, a creature that was either previously unknown to fly anglers or unthinkable to take on fly tackle. The list has included (in the last decade) taimen, golden dorado, and mahseer. Though certainly worthy of angler attention, these quarry require lengthy (and potentially pricey) journeys to faraway lands—Mongolia, Bolivia, and India, respectively. Robert Tomes would like to suggest another species for the "it" list: muskellunge. To find this specimen of *piscine exotica*, you needn't travel to the Amazon or the Himalayas, but to the heartland—in this case, the northern Wisconsin community of Hayward.

"As a boy, I made fishing trips to northern Wisconsin with my dad," Robert began. "In that part of the world, everything is about muskies. It's not only the topic of all angling conversation, but it's the dominant commercial icon—there are muskie bars, muskie tackle shops, muskie motels—it can't be escaped! [The most over-the-top example of muskie-mania is the Shrine to Anglers at Hayward's National Freshwater Fishing Hall of Fame & Museum, which is a half-city-block-long and four-and-a-half-story leaping muskellunge; the structure's open jaw acts as an observation deck that can easily accommodate twenty visitors.] I couldn't help but be intrigued, and my first time out with my dad and a local guide, I landed two fish on a lure called a Mepps Muskie Killer, including a real trophy more than 40 inches. That night at the lodge, they brought out a cake in the shape of a muskie to commemorate my good luck. An old-timer came over and clapped me on the shoulder and said, 'Son, I've been muskie fishing my whole life, I've never caught a keeper.' I knew then that muskies would be part of my life. At the same time, I was fostering a fly-fishing fascination back home in Illinois. An Orvis store opened near my home, and the kindly proprietor there took me under his wing. Soon I was fishing for

215

ROBERT TOMES is the author of *Muskie on the Fly* (www.muskieontheflybook.com), the definitive book on the topic, and is the holder of several, catch-and-release, line-class muskie world records. In addition to his lifelong muskie obsession, he travels regularly around the globe in search of new and exotic fly-fishing challenges. A well-known freelance writer, radio and television guest, and popular speaker on the fly show circuit, he is credited with single handedly creating a minor revolution among fly and conventional anglers alike in search of the elusive "fish of ten thousand casts."

If You Go

▶ **Prime Time:** Robert likes from Memorial Day through the Fourth of July, as the fish are concentrated then, and again from early fall until the close of the season in November, as the fish are feeding aggressively for the long winter.

▶ **Getting There:** Hayward, Wisconsin, is roughly two hours from Eau Claire, which is served by United Airlines (800-864-8331; www.united.com); it's three hours from Minneapolis, which is served by most major carriers.

▶ **Accommodations:** Ross' Teal Lake Lodge (715-462-3631; www.teallake.com) is a popular retreat for muskie anglers, a bit north of Hayward. The Hayward Lakes Visitors & Convention Bureau (800-724-2992; www.haywardlakes.com) highlights a host of other options.

▶ **Guides:** Robert recommends two local guides for muskie fly anglers: Don Larson (715-558-2021; www.pondmonster.com) and Hayward Fly Fishing Company (888-325-2929; www.haywardflyfishingcompany.com).

▶ **Equipment:** A 9-, 10-, or 11-weight rod will work for muskies; the heft is as necessary for the flies you'll toss as the fight. You should come with both floating and sink-tip lines; wire leaders are mandatory. The folks at Hayward Fly Fishing Company can help with flies.

don't feel like you're just flailing away. When you come to Hayward, there's no guarantee you'll catch a muskie, but you'll certainly be in the epicenter of this obsession." Just about wherever you fish in greater Hayward, you'll also connect with the aura of the Northwoods, where the whoosh of an unfurling forward cast is occasionally drowned out by the call of a loon, and calming vistas of majestic pine and birch forests are disturbed by the sudden appearance of a submarine-like apparition cruising the crystalline waters by your craft.

Fly fishing for muskellunge has many attractions, but you should be forewarned that it's not an overly relaxing game. First of all, it usually means blind casting a 9- or 10-weight rod from dawn to dusk, throwing large streamers and poppers, some that would seem better suited to blue-water billfishing than the Northwoods. You'll have to learn about the places muskies like to lie in wait to ambush prey and focus your casting on those places; as Robert pointed out, "It's important to narrow down the options: you simply can't cast to 2 miles of weed beds." You need to resist the temptation to lift your rod when a fish does take and instead use a strip set, like saltwater anglers do. And most important of all, you need the proper mental preparation.

"You need to maintain a cautious optimism that a fish is going to present itself, even though you've been casting for eight hours and haven't seen a thing," Robert advised. "You have to imagine that it's going to happen, have a positive visualization of you hooking, fighting, and landing, and, of course, releasing a muskie. Not everyone can handle that. There are some folks out there who claim expertise, but that's a risky proposition for the fish of ten thousand casts. Muskies are such moody, mysterious creatures that no one can figure out their behavior 100 percent; Sure, there are patterns at times, but no real consistency. You just have to put your time in.

"But when you watch a follow turn into a take, set the hook, and watch that fish cartwheel away or thrash violently on the surface, it's an incredible experience. You've fooled the top-of-the-food-chain fish, and it's an event."

It's no wonder, then, that many of the old guard muskie anglers that thought Robert was "a little bit nuts" when he began fly fishing for muskellunge now are taking up the long rod . . . and that Robert was a keynote speaker at the 16th Annual Chicago Muskie Show, the world's largest exhibition for muskie anglers.

many species with a fly rod. It wasn't too long before I put two and two together: If you can catch trout or tarpon with a fly, you can probably catch muskie. The first time I ever went muskie fishing with my fly rod, I got a nice fish. The visual take, the fight, the aura of having caught this elusive and unpredictable predator on a fly—all of this had a powerful attraction, and it's never, ever gone away."

Alternately described as freshwater barracudas, lake-dwelling tigers, or the fish of ten thousand casts, muskies are the largest members of the pike family. They reside at the top of the food chain in the lakes and rivers they call home and are built for mayhem—long and lithe for quick bursts of speed, with large jaws outfitted with extra-sharp teeth. "You certainly want to handle muskies you catch with care," Robert added. "In the old days, they used to shoot them before bringing them in the boat!" Renowned among devotees for following a bait the entire length of a retrieve before turning away, muskies are picky because they can afford to be; in addition to baitfish, they've been known to eat other game fish, waterfowl, and small mammals. Fish average 30 to 40 inches [10 to 20 pounds], though 50-inch fish—the magic plateau for "trophy" muskies, often eclipsing 40 pounds—are encountered each year. "Anglers today are fortunate to be enjoying a true muskie renaissance," Robert offered. "Catch and release has really caught on. This, combined with other conservation efforts is meaning more and bigger fish." (Fishable populations of muskie are now found well beyond their indigenous range, as far west as Washington and as far south at North Carolina.)

There are several regions that lay claim to the sobriquet of "muskie capital of the world," including Boulder Junction (also in northern Wisconsin) and Clayton, New York, on the St. Lawrence River. Hayward's claim to the title (beyond the Shrine to Anglers) rests in part with its hold on the world-record fish—a 69-pound, 11-ounce monster, caught on the nearby Chippewa Flowage in 1949—and the incredible abundance and variety of muskie waters the region offers. "Hayward has an abundance of Class A action and trophy water," Robert explained. "On action water, you have a significant population of smaller fish and a decent chance of seeing some muskie and maybe even getting a take. On trophy waters, as the name implies, there are some very big fish, but they're few and far between. There are many lakes and flowages around Hayward that hold muskies, and a few rivers as well. For someone fly fishing for muskies for the first time, the rivers and smaller lakes have great appeal. The places where fish might lie are more obvious than on big bodies of water, and the setting is intimate enough that you

OPPOSITE:
Muskie-fly-fishing expert Robert Tomes makes another one of ten thousand casts on the Flambeau River near Hayward, Wisconsin.

217

DESTINATION

49

Published in 2011 by Stewart, Tabori & Chang
An imprint of ABRAMS

Text copyright © 2011 Chris Santella

Photograph credits: Title page and page 66: © Marcelo Dufflocq Williams; Pages 8, 92, and 192:
© Henry Gilbey; Pages 12, 14, 28, 54, and 72: © Ken Morrish — www.flywatertravel.com;
Pages 16, 20, 42, 46, 100, 124, 158, 162, 166, and 208: © Brian O'Keefe; Page 32: © Al Simson;
Page 38: © Brad Harris; Page 50: © Brian Gies — www.flywatertravel.com; Page 62: © Paul Sharman;
Page 80: © Mark B. Hatter; Page 84: © Pat Ford; Page 96: © Naoto Aoki Photography www.naotoaoki.com;
Page 104: © Kirk Anderson; Pages 110 and 204: © Dave McCoy; Page 114: © Joe Healy;
Page 120: © Jim Klug; Page 132: © barryandcathybeck.com; Page 136: © Bob Gillespie; Page 144:
© Scott Taylor; Page 152: © frontierstravel.com; Page 172: © Rok Lustrik; Page 176: © Gerhard Laubscher;
Page 184: © Tim Romano; Page 188: © Kenny Smith; Page 196: © Steffan Jones;
Page 216: © Walter Hodges; Page 220: © John Land Le Coq.

Library of Congress Cataloging-in-Publication Data
Santella, Chris.
Fifty more places to fly fish before you die / Chris Santella.
p. cm.
ISBN 978-1-58479-937-5 (alk. paper)
I. Title.
SH456.S238 2010
799.12'4–dc22
2010048549

Editor: Wesley Royce
Designer: Anna Christian
Production Manager: Tina Cameron
Fifty Places series design by Paul G. Wagner

This book was composed in Interstate, Scala, and Village.

Printed and bound in China
10 9 8 7 6 5 4 3 2 1

Stewart, Tabori & Chang books are available at special discounts when purchased in quantity for premiums
and promotions as well as fundraising or educational use. Special editions can also be created to specification.
For details, contact specialsales@abramsbooks.com or the address below.

THE ART OF BOOKS SINCE 1949

115 West 18th Street
New York, NY 10011
www.abramsbooks.com

JOHN LAND LE COQ is the founder and owner of Fishpond (www.fishpondusa.com), which creates fly-fishing products that stretch the boundaries of traditional product design and set new standards for functionality. Before launching Fishpond, John cofounded Case Logic. He's also a professional photographer and has captured many iconic western images. "Fishpond talks about fly fishing, but it also talks about our water resources, about how people can appreciate them and learn about them and how fragile they are," John has said. "We need to educate people about the importance of these resources and get more people to explore them. Because the more people are passionate about the water and are using it, the stronger the lobby to prevent the other uses, like mining or shale oil, from taking priority and leaving recreational uses at the bottom of the totem pole." John supports many conservation initiatives, including Troubled Waters (www.troubledwatersusa.com), which seeks to end kill-oriented shark tournaments. He lives in Colorado with his daughters.

If You Go

▶ **Prime Time:** From mid-June to late July and early September through October.
▶ **Getting There:** Saratoga is the best Wyoming base for the Upper North Platte. Visitors can fly into Casper, which is served by SkyWest Airlines (as a Delta and United partner) and Allegiant Air (702-505-8888; www.allegiantair.com). It's several hours' drive to Saratoga.
▶ **Accommodations:** There are several hotels in Saratoga, including Wolf Hotel (307-326-5525; www.wolfhotel.com). Elk Hollow Lodge (307-327-6505; www.spuroutfitters.com), 12 miles upstream, caters to anglers.
▶ **Guides/Outfitters:** Outfitters include Four Seasons Anglers (307-721-4047; www.fourseasonsanglers.com) and Stoney Creek Outfitters (307-326-8750; www.fishstoneycreek.com).
▶ **Equipment:** A 5-weight with floating line will work if the wind is down. It's wise to bring a 6- or 7-weight for if or when the wind comes up. Four Seasons Anglers and Stoney Creek Outfitters can guide you toward the best patterns for when you visit.

Crossing into Wyoming, you come into sagebrush country. In places along this stretch, the North Platte has Class IV rapids. In others, it's a meandering meadow stream."

The Upper North Platte is the section of the river from its headwaters in Colorado to the town of Saratoga, Wyoming. Much of the river here is in the shadow of the Medicine Bow Range, where many peaks eclipse 10,000 feet. All 60 miles are designated blue-ribbon trout water and support self-sustaining populations of browns, rainbows, and a smattering of native Snake River cutthroats. Many anglers opt to float the North Platte here, thanks to access issues—and the sheer beauty of the surroundings. "The Northgate Canyon section (which straddles the Colorado–Wyoming border) has some dangerous water in it," John said. "I would advise getting a guide familiar with the water to run that. You'll do some fishing from the boat, but you'll also get out and wade the best water. In June and July, you'll get some great hatches—caddis, green and brown drakes—typical western stuff. In August, you can fish hoppers against the bank; in the fall, you can throw streamers. If I'm fishing the North Platte around Saratoga, I'll try to set aside a day to fish the Encampment River, a little jewel that starts up in the Medicine Bow Wilderness. There's good dry-fly water, good pocket water, good riffles—everything you could want."

If there are two defining elements of the North Platte for John, they are the cottonwoods and the sliver of Americana that the small riverside towns in Wyoming represent. "Nothing characterizes the western landscape for me like the cottonwoods that line so many river bottoms here," John said. "The cottonwoods between Northgate Canyon and Encampment on the North Platte—whether they're green or dead or changing color in the fall—there's nothing like them. And I can't float the river without stopping off to visit the small towns of Saratoga and Encampment; these places are real slices of old-town America. Saratoga is a true cow town. So much of America has become homogenized—even some of the places you go to fish—but Saratoga is the same. Ranching isn't going to change any time soon, so there's no reason for the town to change. There's an old ice cream parlor next to the Hotel Wolf. Even if you don't like ice cream, you have to stop in. Encampment is even smaller. It's a two-block-long logging town, with a little general store. I walked into the store on my last visit. I can still picture the way the canned goods were on display—there's nothing fresh, ranchers need to buy stuff that lasts. There was also a little rusty metal Wonder Bread sign on display. I vividly recall the sound of the store's screen door closing. For me, it says something about the fishing."

UPPER NORTH PLATTE RIVER

RECOMMENDED BY **John Land Le Coq**

"For me, fishing is not about fish," John Le Coq declared. "Fishing is about the experience of place. It takes me to a destination that I normally wouldn't go to. I don't care if I catch a 6-inch fish or a 25-inch fish if I'm visiting an interesting place. One such place for me is Wyoming. There's something about the state that's special. There's the smell of the sagebrush, the sense of remoteness in this sparsely populated place. And there's the light, which is special for me as a photographer. It's hard to describe, but it moves my senses. Somehow, the light lets you know when you've crossed the border from Colorado into Wyoming. A float on the North Platte gives me a quintessential Wyoming experience."

OPPOSITE:
There are great fish in the North Platte, though part of the appeal for John Land Le Coq is the beauty of the cottonwoods.

The North Platte begins in North Park, Colorado (east of Steamboat Springs), at the confluence of Grizzly and Little Grizzly Creeks, and 680 miles later it joins the South Platte in Nebraska. During its 300-mile course through Wyoming, the North Platte has many faces. Many anglers know its two famed tailwater sections—the Miracle Mile and Grey Reef. The former (actually more like 5 to 15 miles depending on flows) rests between Seminoe and Pathfinder Reservoirs and regularly yields fish in the 10-plus-pound category—especially spawning browns in the fall. The Grey Reef stretch, below the Grey Reef and Alcova Reservoirs (about 30 miles southwest of Casper), is celebrated for its rainbows, which average 16 to 20 inches, and can also reach double-digit bulk. (Browns and cutthroat are also here.) While anglers who don't mind double nymph rigs and strong winds will have the opportunity to catch large fish, John is less interested in these tail-waters. He prefers, instead, to fish the upper river. "The relative inaccessibility of the place makes it special," John continued. "You have to work to get there, and that takes a lot of weekend warriors out of the equation. The river in this stretch has a variety of riparian environments. In the Colorado section, it's a meandering, oxbow-laden ranch land river.

221

DESTINATION

50